The Burning Heart

The Burning Heart

Reading the New Testament
with John Main

+>— —<+

Edited by
Gregory Ryan

PAULIST PRESS
New York, N.Y. • Mahwah, N.J.

Published by arrangement with Darton, Longman & Todd Ltd,
London

Published by Paulist Press
997 Macarthur Boulevard
Mahwah, New Jersey 07430

ISBN 0–8091–3724–0

ACKNOWLEDGEMENTS
Death the Inner Journey used by permission of Laurence Freeman OSB
and The World Community for Christian Meditation.
Letters from the Heart: Christian Monasticism and the Renewal of Community by John Main. Copyright © 1982 by John Main. Used with
permission of The Crossroad Publishing Company, New York.
New English Bible © Oxford University Press and Cambridge University Press 1961, 1970.

Phototypeset in 9¹/₂/12¹/₂ pt Palatino by Intype London Ltd
Printed and bound in Great Britain by
Redwood Books, Trowbridge, Wiltshire

Contents

+=- =-+

Foreword

John Main (1926–82) was a Benedictine monk who prayed the Sacred Scriptures not just with his mind but from his heart. His spiritual life was formed by daily *lectio divina*, or prayerful reading of the Scriptures. The Gospel and other New Testament writings – especially those of St Paul – offered daily sustenance to his spiritual development. As a practitioner and teacher of Christian Meditation, John Main found that many New Testament passages illuminated his steps along the path of meditation. His daily periods of meditation nourished his appreciation of the Scriptures, just as his daily reading of the Scriptures nourished his commitment to meditation.

For John Main it was less a paradox and more of a mystery that the words and images of the inspired texts strengthened his commitment to a way of prayer that is wordless and imageless. After all, St Paul taught that we do not know how to pray, but the Spirit prays within us in a manner that is beyond words and beyond images. Meditation is just such a way of prayer.

After John Main's death in 1982, his personal copy of the New Testament was found to have a number of passages marked by him. These passages had frequently formed the basis for the Monday and Tuesday evening conferences he had given to those who came to his monastery – first in London and then in Montreal – to learn to meditate. Those

Scripture passages, along with excerpts from his reflections on them, form the text of this book.

I think you will find that John Main's words are enlightened and enlightening and that they will lead you to a fresh and renewed appreciation of Scripture texts which may have become all-too-familiar and taken for granted. Along with the practice of *lectio divina*, John Main recommended the daily practice of meditation so that we would not find ourselves just *talking to* God, or *thinking about* God, but *being with* God.

John Main's eloquent words encourage us in our daily commitment to Christian Meditation as we journey back to the Father with Christ in the Spirit in silence, stillness and simplicity. The Scripture passages and the teachings of John Main presented in this book will lead you to the depths of your heart where you will find immeasurable peace and abiding joy awaiting you.

Gregory Ryan
Benedictine Oblate,
The World Community for Christian Meditation
Pentecost 1996

Introduction

━┿━   ━┿━

In the first few centuries of Christianity the initiation into the 'new way' of the faith was a momentous leap for the individual and his or her family. It involved joining a marginalised and politically suspect religious group that was often regarded as socially dangerous as well as intellectually contemptible. Preparing for the solemn initiatory rite of baptism, which was also an initiation to the eucharistic table, was a long, carefully monitored process of study and prayer. When it finally happened, baptism was an initiation that expressed – sacramentalised – the whole process of personal conversion.

Conversion, then as now, is not just a matter of changing your opinions or acquiring a new spiritual credit card. It is a revolution in the deep structures of the personality that, if it is genuine, goes on for the rest of your life. St Benedict recognised this when he had his monks take a lifelong vow of conversion. Their vows, symbolising the laws of all spiritual life, committed them not only to stability and rootedness but also to constant change. All growth, physical, psychological or spiritual, requires this combination of fixity and flexibility, just as a tree grows by sinking its roots deeper and pushing its branches higher.

The basic truths of conversion are the same today as in the past. Our circumstances differ from those of the early Christians although we are increasingly able to sympathise with their experience of being a marginal minority group as the institutional forms of the Churches dissolve around us. We differ from the Early Church inasmuch as our conversion is likely to begin many years after we are baptised and after we have been receiving communion as a matter of course for a long time. But we are beginning to resemble the early Christians in that as the old mediaeval power-systems of the Church and the mentalities which they engender give way, a new meaning of being Christian is being formed. The historical roles and identities of bishops, priests, ministers and laity are being rewritten. The relationship of Christianity to the other faiths is losing its old intolerance except among the fundamentalists. And Christians are once again tasting the bittersweetness of mockery and misrepresentation in the media.

A great benefit of these changes for the modern Christian is the, not so much *re*-discovery, as *first* discovery for so many of the mysteries of their faith. This means that once conversion has really begun, the words of Scripture and the meaning of the rituals of worship, like the Eucharist, come alive with a power, a relevance and a personal richness that fills one with surprise, wonder, delight and gratitude.

For this renewal of faith in personal experience a new kind of initiation is demanded, deeper and more interior than the earlier rituals but revealing their original meaning. Whereas baptism, confirmation and the Eucharist are, in a sense, formal or external signs of initiation into the Church as the Body of Christ, there is also another, quieter and more individual initiation into the Mind of Christ. This happens rather than being performed. It is an initiation into an experience of prayer in the heart rather than the mind alone. It is characterised by silence and stillness and a profound trust in the love of God, rather than by words, gestures or petitions. This contemplative initiation is being undergone by many Christians today.

This initiation into the deeper meanings of the faith and into the experience of them restores many of the lost arts of the Christian life – such as the art of reading Scripture or of celebrating the Eucharist. For many people the ancient discipline of meditation which John Main recognised in the early Christian monastic teachings and then distilled into a simple discipline of daily contemplative practice for all, has become a powerful path into this spiritual initiation.

Although John Main's short but intense ministry of teaching meditation concentrated on this missing contemplative dimension in Christianity, he well knew that there are other important dimensions and ways of prayer. As a monk he was daily immersed in Scripture through the monastic office and chant of the monastery and he was nourished regularly by the celebration of the Eucharist. Once he had recovered the practice of meditation in his own life, he saw how all these diverse dimensions of prayer were in fact interdependent and formed a unity which reached its fullness in the prayer of Jesus himself. John Main and his communities prepared for meditation by the celebration of the Divine Office, with its rich weaving of Old and New Testament Scripture. When they celebrated the Eucharist a half-hour period of meditation followed the communion before the concluding prayer and blessing. It was this rediscovery of the inter-connectedness of all forms of prayer in the Mind and Heart of the praying Christ that meditation makes so richly possible.

Deep in the modern psyche there is a split between the sacred and the secular. It affects religious people no less than those who reject all belief. The consequence of this divided psyche is a split vision of reality. And the results of this in turn are wide-ranging and inestimable both psychologically and sociologically. One law seems to rule us in politics, business and entertainment while quite another operates in church and private life. A daily practice of meditation such as John Main recommended has had a remarkable result in the lives of many people who have felt the pain and anxiety of this inner and outer division. Meditation heals the terrible wound that seems to cut off such large parts of our life from the healing and vivifying power of the sacred. Imperceptibly, like the seed in the ground which, as Jesus said, grows 'we know not how' and which symbolises the Kingdom, the mantra in the times of meditation unifies our personalities and inner being. Meditation reveals the inner purpose and direction of our lives by enlightening us as to the interdependent unity which exists between us and nature and us and the rest of the human family.

John Main knew, of course, that the way of the mantra which he and his community taught, was not the only way into the contemplative depths of the Christian life. But he knew that a way was needed because no way was being taught, and that discipline was demanded by any way that will bear fruit in a person's spiritual life. He understood also that the simplicity of the way of meditation which he recovered from the early Christian was its great contemporary relevance and attraction. Simplicity is what we need and hunger for. It is the immediate goal of all spiritual practice.

This book of John Main's use of Scripture in his teaching of meditation has been elegantly and usefully edited by Gregory Ryan. For anyone still waiting to begin a contemplative practice of prayer these readings and their commentaries will offer insight into how the Word is illuminated by silence and emerges from silence. For anyone already meditating this book will be another valuable encouragement for the perseverance which is necessary to bring us all to the fullness of life which Jesus came to make available to us.

This small book, read prayerfully and used as a way to

prepare for or to conclude a period of meditation in which the whole person, body, mind and spirit, becomes deeply and attentively silent, will make the daily journey to the heart lighter and brighter.

Laurence Freeman osb
International Centre,
The World Community for Christian Meditation
London, May 1996

How to Meditate

Sit down. Sit still and upright. Close your eyes lightly. Sit relaxed but alert. Silently, interiorly begin to say a single word. We recommend the prayer-phrase *'maranatha'*. Recite it as four syllables of equal length. Listen to it as you say it, gently but continuously. Do not think or imagine anything – spiritual or otherwise. If thoughts and images come, these are distractions at the time of meditation, so keep returning to simply saying the word. Meditate each morning and evening for between 20 and 30 minutes.

The Practice of Lectio Divina

※ ※

This book is not meant to replace your twice-daily periods of meditation. Neither is it meant to be read from beginning to end as a kind of intellectual exercise. In the centuries-old tradition of *lectio divina* – which is Latin for *sacred reading* – I would suggest that, before or after your morning or evening meditation, you read just one of the selections. After reading it one time, you may want to go back, either then or later, and spend 15 or 20 minutes reverently turning the passage over in your heart. Read slowly and lovingly, pausing whenever the words draw you into silence. Close your eyes and experience the meaning of the words. But even more, experience the Presence found in them. Let the Reality of the words become more and more a part of your being.

During the time of *lectio*, the historical setting of the passage is not as important as the place it has in *your* life *now*. In a real sense, you are not the same person you were ten or five or even one year ago. Since you are always a 'new person' your response to the Word will never be the same. You may find yourself making acts of the will to conform your life more to the message of the text. One day you may rest in a deep peace. Another day you may be aware of tension, anger or sorrow. These feelings should not cause any anxiety because they are all part of God's healing action at work in you. In time, you will learn to accept yourself as a work-in-progress, and your growing appreciation for the Living Word of God will lead you to a life of constant wonder, gratitude and love.

Abbreviations

Books used by John Main in this text.

CM	Christian Meditation
CL	Community of Love
DJ	Death the Inner Journey
LH	Letters from the Heart
MC	Moment of Christ
PC	The Present Christ
WU	The Way of Unknowing
WS	Word Into Silence
WF	Word Made Flesh

Reading the New Testament
with John Main

+= =+

When we look at the New Testament, at least when we look at it with eyes enlightened by the spirit of Christ burning in our hearts, we cannot but become intoxicated, amazed at the sheer wonder of the destiny that is given to each of us. But, we must always remember that the condition of being open to this, and of responding to our destiny, is always simplicity, poverty of spirit. It means we are invited by the same destiny to leave behind all complexity, all desire to possess God or to possess spiritual knowledge and to tread the narrow way of dispossession. We require faithfulness. We learn to be faithful by being simply faithful to the daily times of meditation and, during the meditation, to the saying of the mantra.

(WU, p.3)

The Gospel According to Saint Matthew

+= =+

'You are light for all the world. A town that stands on a hill cannot be hidden. When a lamp is lit, it is not put under the meal-tub, but on the lamp-stand, where it gives light to everyone in the house. And you, like the lamp, must shed light among your fellows, so that, when they see the good you do, they may give praise to your Father in heaven.' (Matt. 5: 14–16)

There is only one way to do this and it is the essential means of shedding the light with which the Church is entrusted upon every one in the house. This is the way of prayer. The means, in this matter as in all, have to be conformable to the end. Our Christian communities do not exist for themselves, but for others and ultimately for the Other. In our prayer we have to discover ourselves existing for the Other because it is in prayer that we experience ourselves being created and sustained by Him. (WS, p.76)

+= =+

'In your prayers do not go babbling on like the heathen, who imagine the more they say the more likely they are to be heard. Do not imitate them. Your Father knows what your needs are before you ask him. This is how you should pray . . .' (Matt. 6: 7–9)

As I have suggested, prayer is not a matter of talking to God, but of listening to Him, or being with Him. It is this simple understanding of prayer that lies behind John Cassian's advice that if we want to pray, to listen, we must become quiet and still, by reciting a short verse over and over again. Cassian received this method as something which was an old, established tradition in his own day and it is an enduring universal tradition. A thousand years after Cassian, the English author of *The Cloud of Unknowing* recommends the repetition of a little word: 'We must pray in the height, depth, length, and breadth of our spirit, not in many words but in a little word.' (WS, p.10)

The pilgrimage of prayer is followed between . . . two dead ends of illusion: 'talking your problems over' [with God] is always likely to lead you deeper into ego fixation, and drifting in an undisciplined self-observation is likely to isolate you more effectively from God, from others, from yourself. This is why the simplicity and the poverty of the mantra is so vital to the pilgrimage. In saying it with fidelity we are doing all we are called to do, which is to turn from self. The rest we leave to the free gift of God, without desire or expectation. We begin in faith. We continue in faith. In faith we arrive. Our opportunity and our responsibility is to be self-emptying disciples of our Master. (LH, p.95)

+►— —◄+

'Set your mind on God's Kingdom and his justice before everything else, and all the rest will come to you as well.' (Matt. 6: 33)

The proper ordering of our external activities can only be achieved once we have re-established conscious contact with the centre of all these activities and concerns. This centre is the aim of our meditation. It is the centre of our being. In St Teresa's words, 'God is the centre of the soul.' When our access to this centre is opened up, the Kingdom of God is established in our hearts. That Kingdom is nothing less than the present power and all-pervasive life of God Himself permeating all creation . . . (WS, pp.66–7)

＋ ＋

And this is another parable that he put before them: 'The kingdom of Heaven is like a mustard-seed, which a man took and sowed in his field. As a seed, mustard is smaller than any other; but when it has grown it is bigger than any garden-plant; it becomes a tree, big enough for the birds to come and roost among its branches.' (Matt. 13: 31–33)

The experience of transcendence . . . occurs within the nature of things – our nature – the parables of the Kingdom show that the essence of experience is natural growth. A small mustard-seed grows into a tree big enough for the birds to come and roost in its branches. To try to make it grow faster or slower would be absurd and counterproductive. It is the same when we experience the growth of the Kingdom in our hearts as we follow the journey of meditation. Day by day we let the husk of the ego drop away and like a seed we die to self that we may fulfil the destiny that is our true meaning, that the potential of life within us may come to full fruition. (LH, pp.70–71)

＋ ＋

'The kingdom of Heaven is like treasure lying buried in a field. The man who found it, buried it again; and for sheer joy went and sold everything he had, and bought that field.' (Matt. 13: 44)

There are no half measures. You can't decide to do a bit of meditation. The option is to meditate and to root your life in reality. The reality is the reality of liberty – that you are freed to be, and to be fully, every moment of your life. As far as I can understand it, that is what the Gospel is about. That is what Christian prayer is about. A commitment to life, a commitment to *eternal* life. Jesus taught that the kingdom of Heaven is here and now. What we have to do is to be open to it, which is to be committed to it. (MC, p.32)

+— —+

'Stay awake, and pray that you may be spared the test.' (Matt. 26: 41)

[John] Cassian brought the answer to the West from the ancient tradition of Christian prayer. By knowing ourselves to be poor and by deepening in prayer our experience of poverty in complete self-renunciation. The simple practical means he teaches is the unceasing use of the mantra. He wrote that the Christian has as his principal aim the realisation of the kingdom of God, the power of the Spirit of Jesus in his heart. But we cannot achieve this by our own efforts or think our way into it and so we have a simpler more immediate goal which he calls 'purity of heart'. This is all we should concern ourselves with, he teaches. The rest will be given to us. And the way to purity of heart, to full and clear awareness, is the way of poverty, the 'grand poverty' of the mantra. (WS, p.63)

+— —+

'And be assured, I am with you always, to the end of time.' (Matt. 28: 20)

Learning to pray is learning to live as fully as possible in the present moment. In meditation we seek to enter as fully as we can into the now, and in entering into the now to live as fully as possible with the now-risen and ever-loving Lord Jesus. To be thus fully committed to the present moment is to find ourselves, to enter into ourselves, to dwell within ourselves; and this we do by renouncing thought and image. In meditation we are not thinking about the past, neither our own past nor anyone else's. In meditation we are wholly inserted into the present, and there we live to the fullness of our capability, our consciousness expanding as we entertain the Lord of Life. The experience of this being wholly conscious is an experience of unity and simplicity. (WS, p.22)

The Gospel According to Saint Mark

+=— =—+

'Anyone who wishes to be a follower of mine must leave self behind.' (Mark 8: 34)

The faithful saying of our mantra is our response to this call of Jesus. It is work – the work of God. Above all, meditation is an all-out onslaught on egoism, on isolation and on sadness. It is an affirmation of consciousness and life through the experience of love. The Christian vision demands a community that is created and vitalised in the mind of Christ. The message this community must communicate is that it is possible for all of us to become alive with the life of Christ. It is not only possible, it is the destiny of each one of us. (PC, p.88)

+=— =—+

He sat down with the Twelve, and said to them, 'If anyone wants to be first, he must make himself last of all and servant of all.' (Mark 9: 35)

As we advance into the silence [of meditation] we begin to experience the true meaning of the words of Jesus ... It requires nerve to become really quiet. To learn just to say the mantra and turn away from all thought requires courage. But as we persevere we discover that the poverty of the mantra leads us to a really radical simplicity that makes this courage possible, for we are capable of greater courage than we usually believe of ourselves. But meditation is the prayer of faith, because we have to leave ourselves behind before the Other appears and with no pre-packaged guarantee that He will appear. The essence of poverty consists in this risk of annihilation. This is the leap of faith from ourselves to the Other. This is the risk involved in all loving. (WS, p.23)

+━━ ━━+

'I tell you, whoever does not accept the kingdom of God like a child will never enter it.' (Mark 10: 15)

What we must do is to begin to meditate, to begin to open ourselves up to the love of God and its power. To do this, all we need to do is to begin to say the mantra, lovingly and in a deep spirit of faith. (WS, p.17)

The children who come to our monastery to meditate are a marvellous witness of the naturalness of this way of meditation. They are a real example for the adults who come. They show the essentially childlike quality that we need to tread the way ... It is a simple way. Its simplicity is its great challenge to us because we are trained to seek the truth, for accuracy, only in complexity. It is a *simple* but not necessarily *easy* way. It requires trust and perhaps indeed a certain recklessness to begin and it requires courage to persevere but all we have to lose are our own limitations. (DJ, p.4)

+━━ ━━+

Jesus said to him, 'What do you want me to do for you?' 'Master,' the blind man answered, 'I want my sight back.' Jesus said to him, 'Go; your faith has cured you.' (Mark 10: 51)

We need the wisdom to search into the depths of things. We also need a deepening sensitivity to a dimension of reality which can only be revealed to those who want to see, who are humble enough to cry out with the blind beggar of the Gospel . . . It is only the blindly arrogant who claim to see enough. Those who are beginning to see are aware of how much more their vision of faith needs to be purified. They know that no man can see God and live. The more we see him the further our self-consciousness contracts and our ego evaporates. To see God is to be absorbed into him. To have the 'eye' of our heart opened by the process of his love is to lose our very sense of the 'I' who sees. This is the sensitivity, the delicacy of spiritual refinement we need in order to see the risen Christ. It is the gentle delicacy that follows the cataclysm of death. It is the spirit of fully selfless love that does not flinch from being transformed into the beloved. (PC, p.91)

The Gospel According to
Saint Luke

+>= =<+

His mother treasured up all these things in her heart.
(Luke 2: 51)

[Mary's] silence possesses a radiant creativity and consciousness because it is so clearly the positive, affirmative
silence of other-centredness. She is not retreating from
reality into a private netherworld but is attendant upon the
emergence of the grand design of her life and the
full revelation of its meaning. Her transcendence of self
is the archetypal other-centredness of a mother's love
for her child: a relationship that captured the Jewish
religious imagination long before, both as an expression of
God's unfailing love of human beings and of their
dependence on God. The reality of such a relationship is
only revealed in silence. And it is only in silence and
through silence that we can interiorise what is beyond our
comprehension and apprehend the power of a design larger
than ourselves: it is the medium of *transcendence*. (CL, p.169)

+>= =<+

And from time to time he would withdraw to lonely
places for prayer ... During this time he went out one
day into the hills to pray, and spent the night in prayer
to God. (Luke 5: 16; 6: 12)

I could use all the words in our vocabulary to tell you about the eternal silence of God that dwells within our innermost being, the silence of pure creation. I could say how important that silence is because in it you hear your own name spoken clearly and unmistakably for the first time. You come to know who you are. Yet all these words would fail to convey the experience itself – an experience of unself-conscious liberty in the creating presence of God.

To learn to be silent is to say your mantra and to keep saying it. So do not fear to leave your thoughts behind. Do not go back to your ideas or imagination. Leave them to one side and say your word. We are not alone in doing this . . .

When we meditate in this tradition we enter into this same silence and it makes us one with Jesus in God. (WF, pp.54, 53)

+≡— —≡+

'The seed in good soil represents those who bring a good and honest heart to the hearing of the word, hold it fast, and by their perseverance yield a harvest.' (Luke 8: 15)

Meditation is a universal means to lead us to reality. The reality that we are, the reality that our neighbour is, the reality that history is and the ultimate reality, the reality that is God. Meditation is the means open to everyone who would encounter the Spirit in their own heart. And so I want to encourage each one of you to persevere in meditation. Courage is what we need, the courage above all to abandon all images, especially the images that we have of ourselves, which are the principle stumbling block. The way to abandon all those images is to say our word with deepening fidelity. To enter our own selfhood is to enter into God. This is the call given to each one of us, to know

ourselves in God. It is an astonishing destiny and it has
been given to us in Jesus to know that destiny. Our life's
task is to respond to it, in utter seriousness and with total
joy. So listen to the word of the tradition. Hold fast to it
and reap the harvest of eternal love. (WU, pp.78–9)

+〓 〓+

> And to all he said, 'If anyone wishes to be a follower of
> mine, he must leave self behind; day after day he must
> take up his cross, and come with me.' (Luke 9: 23)

To that call we respond when we meditate every day. We
mislead ourselves and others if we try to play down the
extremity of the Christian vocation and the total demand it
makes. If we have been directed by the Spirit to undertake
this pilgrimage, and every Christian is chosen to do so, then
it must be with the mature understanding of what is at
stake. As we enter the silence within us, having allowed
ourselves to become aware of its presence in the first place,
we are entering a void in which we are unmade. We cannot
remain the person we were or thought we were. But we
are, in fact, not being destroyed but awakened to the eternally fresh source of our being. We become aware that we
are being created, that we are springing from the Creator's
hand and returning to Him in love. (WS, pp.31–2)

+〓 〓+

> 'Think of the lilies: they neither spin nor weave; yet I
> tell you, even Solomon in all his splendour was not
> attired like one of these. But if that is how God clothes
> the grass, which is growing in the field today, and
> tomorrow is thrown on the stove, how much more will
> he clothe you! How little faith you have! And so you are
> not to set your mind on food and drink; you are not to

worry. For all these are things for the heathen to run
after; but you have a Father who knows that you need
them. No, you must set your mind upon his kingdom,
and all the rest will come to you as well.' (Luke 12:
27–31)

The call to meditate is an invitation to stop leading our
lives on the basis of second-hand evidence. It is a call to
each one of us to come to grips with our spiritual capacity
and so to discover for ourselves the astonishing richness of
the human capacity that is anchored in the divine reality,
in the divine life-power. And it is also an invitation to be
simply open to that power, to be energised by it and to
be swept along by it, into the depths of the divine reality
itself. (HC, p.29)

＊＊＊

'The kingdom of God is among you.' (Luke 17: 21)

To face death with a hope that makes us fully human and
to live with a spirit of liberty and joy in being we must find
this centre in time. We must learn to be one with this centre,
which is another way of saying we must find our real selves.
The search in our tradition is conducted in stillness, in
silence and with discipline. The search is not in the first
place an elaboration of concepts. It is not in the first place
an intellectual penetration of the mystery. In the first
place the search is conducted simply be allowing ourselves
to be. (DJ, p.1)

＊＊＊

They even brought babies for him to touch. When the
disciples saw them they rebuked them, but Jesus called
for the children and said, 'Let the little ones come to me;

do not try to stop them; for the kingdom of God belongs
to such as these. I tell you that whosoever does not
accept the kingdom of God like a child will never enter
it.' (Luke 18: 15–17)

Learning to meditate is learning to unlearn. The big problem
that faces anyone who starts to meditate is the simplicity
of it. God is One. And Christian prayer has been described
as the way of one-ing, becoming one with the One who is
One. The problem we face is to leave complexity behind.
We are used to complexity because we are brought up to
believe that the more perfect the technique, the more stun-
ning will be the result. The perfecting of techniques
increases complexity. The perfecting of a discipline leads to
simplicity. And Jesus tells us to become simple, to become
childlike. Meditation is the way of rediscovering our
innate, childlike sense of wonder. Christian prayer is a state
of innocence. When we meditate we go beyond desire,
beyond possessiveness, beyond self-importance, beyond all
sources of guilt and complexity. So the first thing you must
learn when you set out on the pilgrimage of meditation is
to listen to the message with the simplicity of a child. God
is One. And the extraordinary thing about the Christian
proclamation is that our vocation is to be one with him, in
him and through him. (WU, p.38)

＋━ ━＋

When he rose from prayer and came to the disciples he
found them asleep, worn out by grief. 'Why are you
sleeping?' he said. 'Rise and pray that you may be spared
the test.' (Luke 22: 45–6)

This episode from the Gospels reveals Jesus as the great
master of prayer. His call to his disciples and to us is a call
to full wakefulness. Falling asleep is the perennial temp-

tation for the man or woman of prayer. Cassian spoke of the principal dangers in entering true prayer in phrases such as the 'perilous peace' and the 'fatal sleep' [*Conf.* 4: 7, 10: 8]. Once a person has entered into this nether world it is no easy task to summon them back to life and enlightenment. Jesus returned to his disciples in the garden and three times found them sleeping. (CL, p.107)

The Gospel According to
Saint John

+=─ ─=+

Through him all things came to be; no single thing was
created without him. (John 1: 3)

... All things and all men return to the Father through the
Son ... So just as He is the prime and ultimate expression
of the Father, Jesus is also the hinge upon which the universe and all being swings back to the Father, its source. It
is through our incorporation in the body of Christ in this
swing-back to the Father that we are destined to be accepted
as sons of God. (WS, p.34)

+=─ ─=+

'The time approaches, indeed it is already here, when
those who are real worshippers will worship the Father
in spirit and in truth. Such are the worshippers whom
the Father wants. God is spirit, and those who worship
him must worship in spirit and truth.' (John 4: 23–4)

Meditation is the way of making full contact with your own
spirit, of making full contact with truth. Remember the Way.
Say your mantra from the beginning to the end. Meditate
every morning and every evening, faithfully, simply and
humbly. Contemplation consists in the simple enjoyment of
the truth. (MC, p.101)

+=─ ─=+

'In very truth, anyone who gives heed to what I say and
puts his trust in him who sent me has hold of eternal life,
and does not come up for judgement, but has already
passed from death to life.' (John 5: 24)

That is the truth of the Gospel that each of us is invited not
just to read, but to live. The Gospel of Jesus is about living.
It is about life and all of us are invited to live our lives not,
as it were, at fifty or sixty percent of our potential, but at a
hundred percent: to live life with fullness. The witness of
the Gospel proclaims that this is only possible for any of us
if we are fully in touch with our life-source, which is the
source of all life, the Divine energy. Jesus spoke to 'anyone
who gives heed to what I say'. We have to learn to *listen* to
him, to listen deeply to the invitation to live our lives to the
full and so to be filled with divine power. We have to listen
with the fullness of our own being, profoundly, totally. That
is why the silence of meditation is so important and why
each of us, through our own experience as we continue to
meditate, discovers that silence is so precious a value in
our lives in general. Silence also touches our common life
together so that we can share a sense of the mysterious
power both in our midst and beyond us. (WU, p.35)

Meditation is focused right in the heart, right in the centre
of the Christian mystery. And the Christian mystery can
only be penetrated if we enter into the mystery of death
and resurrection . . .

What we do in meditation and in the life-long process of
meditation is to refine our perception down to the single
focal point which is Christ. Christ is our way, our goal, our
guide. But he is our goal only in the sense that once we are
wholly with him, wholly at one with him, we pass with
him to the Father. In meditation we come to that necessary
single-pointedness and find it is Christ. (MC, p.13)

⊶   ⊷

'I am the light of the world. No follower of mine shall wander in the dark; he shall have the light of life.' (John 8: 12)

In beginning to meditate we are declaring a courageous acceptance of this invitation of Jesus and we enter into our meditation on each occasion as the twin process of vitalisation and enlightenment. (WS, p.19)

✥ ✥

Turning to the Jews who had believed him, Jesus said, 'If you dwell within the revelation I have brought, you are indeed my disciples; you shall know the truth, and the truth will set you free.' (John 8: 31–2)

Meditation is entering into that experience of being free for God, transcending desire, sin, leaving it behind; transcending ego, leaving it behind, so that the whole of our being is utterly available to God. It is in that profound availability that we become ourselves ... Meditation is simply dwelling within the revelation, dwelling within the vision of God. (MC, pp.16–17)

✥ ✥

'I have come that men may have life, and may have it in all its fullness.' (John 10: 10).

As we die to the ego we rise to a way of life that astonishes us with its infinite richness, its wonder and, above all, with its absolute liberty of spirit. Meditation is a healing process. What is healed is the essential wound we all have: the wound of the divided self that separates us from ourselves, from others, from God – and so from our own full potential. (DJ, p.4)

✥ ✥

> 'When a man believes in me, he believes in him who
> sent me rather than in me.' (John 12: 44)

This is the real meaning of faith: openness, perseverance in
wakefulness, commitment to the pilgrimage. The word for
faith (*pistis*) common in the Gospel sayings of Jesus nowhere
in his teachings meant 'belief' or 'conviction'. It carries
instead the sense of 'trust', 'faithfulness', personal loyalty.
To follow Jesus was not merely to have an intellectual
understanding about him but to experience his personal
revelation and the dimension of spirit his person opened
for us – to experience this at the centre of our lives to the
point of union with him and so ultimately with the
Father . . . (LH, p.57)

The openness and steadiness of faith in Jesus transcends
every human limitation separating us from the Father's
love, the source and goal of our being. No one approaches
the Father except through Jesus. He is the Way. But we do
not enter the Way, pursue the pilgrimage, except through
faith. For St Paul faith, or our open-hearted turning towards
the Lord, was the fundamental quality of the Christian
experience, without which the Gospel cannot save. It is,
indeed, as fundamental as our very creation because,
although we can say now that we *exist*, we cannot say that
we are in full *being* until we have entered into fully conscious relationship, until we have turned freely toward God
and thereby reciprocated love, completed the cycle of love.
In the spiritual dimension we become the person we are
called to be in Christ only by that gift of ourselves, that
other-centredness that is the dynamic of faith . . . (CL,
pp.108–9)

'If you love me you will obey my commands; and I will
ask the Father, and he will give you another to be your
Advocate, who will be with you for ever – the Spirit of
truth. The world cannot receive him, because the world
neither sees nor knows him; but you know him, because
he dwells with you and is in you. I will not leave you
bereft; I am coming back to you. In a little while the
world will see me no longer, but you will see me; because
I live, you too will live; then you will know that I am in
my Father, and you in me and I in you.' (John 14: 15–20)

The greatest of all paradoxes is contained in these words
which are among the most extraordinary ever composed. In
them we see the mystery of personal being within universal
unity . . .

We know ourselves loved and so we love. Meditation is
concerned with completing this cycle of love. By our openness to the Spirit who dwells in our hearts, and who in
silence is loving to all, we begin the journey of faith. We
end in faith because there is always a new beginning to the
eternal dance of being-in-love. (WF, pp.29, 30)

⊷ ⊶

'He who dwells in me, as I dwell in him, bears much
fruit; for apart from me you can do nothing . . . If you
dwell in me, and my words dwell in you, ask what
you will, and you shall have it. This is my Father's glory,
that you may bear fruit in plenty and so be my disciples.
As the Father has loved me, so I have loved you. Dwell
in my love. If you heed my commands, you will dwell in
my love, as I have heeded my Father's commands and
dwell in his love.' (John 15: 5, 7–10)

Relationship, community and authentic progress are possible because each person possesses within the energy and

consciousness necessary to defeat isolation, selfishness and death. Through our daily meditation we become one with this divine energy and consciousness. It is the power of the Spirit to expand us into generosity, life and love, indeed into eternal, which means limitless, life. (WF, p.44)

+>— —<+

'I call you servants no longer; a servant does not know what his master is about. I have called you friends, because I have disclosed to you everything that I heard from my Father.' (John 15: 15)

Jesus explained His own mission as the proclamation of the Father: the revelation to men of the person whom He encountered in the depths of His own human heart. His union with men, His calling us friends and brothers, His loving all-embracing universalisation through the Spirit: all these considerations serve to confirm what He Himself assured us of, that we are called to the same knowledge and the same communion with the Father, the same completion and verification of our being that He enjoyed as man and communicates to us as the incarnate Word. When He sends the Spirit into our hearts, Jesus transmits to us everything that He receives from the Father . . . (WS, p.45)

+>— —<+

'You did not choose me: I chose you . . . This is my commandment to you: love one another.' (John 15: 16, 17)

Christian discipleship is lived detachment and loving othercentredness. And meditation begins with a call that awakens us out of the coma of self-preoccupation. We are called, we are chosen. Meditation is our response to that call from the deepest centre of our awakened consciousness . . .

In meditation by letting go, by openness to the centre of being we learn how to love. (HC, p.75)

+— —+

'All that the Father has is mine,' (John 16: 15) 'I have disclosed to you everything that I heard from the Father.' (John 15: 15)

It is as a result of this oneness of Father and Son and of the Son's oneness with us that we are able to stand in the truth. The innate restlessness of man in his condition of growth is the consequence of his having an expanding capacity to be in the truth, to be one with the truth. He is impelled by the inner expansiveness of his own being to align himself to his destiny and to enter the simplicity of the egoless state which growth demands – the need to let go of the past and to venture upon what is to come without desire or resistance. We are restless for the truth; above all, the truth of our own being, for there we can be sure we are not encountering an image or theory of truth, but truth incarnate – what we instinctively recognise as reality. The revelation of the Father to us occurs in union with the consciousness of Jesus is the fundamental authenticity of human life. (PC, p.53)

+— —+

She turned around and saw Jesus standing there, but did not recognise him . . . Jesus said, 'Mary!' She turned to him and said, 'Rabbuni!' (which is Hebrew for 'My Master'). (John 20: 14–16)

In the profoundly real and symbolic atmosphere of this

encounter there is a marvellously condensed account of the human response to the Resurrection. We hear and see the good news, but until the moment that it engages our absolute attention, by name, we fail to recognise it. When we do, all thought of self evaporates in the overwhelming joy of the reality so much greater than us, that can call us to itself. Mary is described as 'turning' twice, in this brief episode. For all of us there is this two-fold conversion that unfolds throughout a lifetime, the total conversion that demands absolute harmony of mind and heart. (PC, p.90)

The Letter of Saint Paul
to the Romans

✜━ ━✜

> For all alike have sinned, and are deprived of the divine splendour, and all are justified by God's free grace alone, through his act of liberation in the person of Christ Jesus. (Rom. 3: 23–4)

This is the faith our meditation is founded on; entering into that liberty, accepting that act of liberation and being made utterly free. Passing beyond all limitation, we are still, as we become one with God, in total harmony with him. That is the purpose of our meditation. This is the way and the time is now. (HC, p.81)

✜━ ━✜

> Now that we have been justified through faith, let us continue at peace with God through our Lord Jesus Christ, through whom we have been allowed to enter the sphere of God's grace, where we now stand. Let us exult in the hope of the divine splendour that is to be ours. (Rom. 5: 1–2)

You will see that the main effect of this passage is to draw our attention to what condition we are in now, to draw our minds into steady concentration on the present moment.

The extraordinary dynamism of these words and the whole of St Paul's writing is that the marvel, the splendour, the unimaginable reality of the condition we are in here and now is so overwhelming that we can hardly keep our concentration steady. We have been allowed to enter the sphere of God's grace where we now stand. Jesus has blazed the trail for us and through His own experience has incorporated us in His present state which is His glorious communion with the Father in His risen life, a life that now pervades the whole of creation. We stand in the sphere of God's grace because we are where He is and He is where we are. We are in Him and His Spirit is in us. (WS, pp.74–5)

+━ ━+

Therefore, now that we have been justified through faith, let us continue at peace with God through our Lord Jesus Christ, through whom we have been allowed to enter the sphere of God's grace, where we now stand. Let us exult in the hope of the divine splendour that is to be ours . . . because God's love has flooded our inmost heart through the Holy Spirit he has given us. (Rom. 5: 1–5)

Just think about this language for a moment and consider the quite staggering claim it is making . . . St Paul was no mere theorist . . . His great conviction is that the central reality of our Christian faith is the sending of the Spirit of Jesus; indeed our faith is a living faith precisely because the living Spirit of God dwells within us, giving new life to our mortal bodies.

The all-important aim in Christian meditation is to allow God's mysterious and silent presence within us to become more and more not only *a* reality, but *the* reality in our lives; to let it become that reality which gives meaning, shape and purpose to everything we do, to everything we are. (WS, p.3)

+━ ━+

This proof is the ground of hope. Such a hope is no
mockery, because God's love has flooded our inmost
heart through the Holy Spirit he has given us.
(Rom. 5: 4–5)

... The presence of Jesus within us, His Holy Spirit, calls
out to us to become fully conscious of this level of our
being. In the twinkling of an eye, we awaken to ourselves,
to the Spirit dwelling in us, and thence to consciousness of
the communion within God Himself in which we are called
to share. And so, we awaken not to a platonic aloneness
but to a complete communion of all beings in Being itself.
(WS, p.38)

+━━ ━━+

By baptism we were buried with him, and lay dead, in
order that, as Christ was raised from the dead in the
splendour of the Father, so also we might set our feet
upon the new path of life. (Rom. 6: 4)

To know this is to be a Christian, not just a member of a
church or sect but a joyful personal disciple. It is to know
that this new path of life is already opened up for us
because of the energies set free among all humanity by the
Resurrection. From our point of view we may see only
the same tired, worn, old paths but if this Resurrection
energy has touched us, if we have touched it in our
hearts, the new path of life stands out brilliant and
dominant, transcending all the old ways. As the snows
of winter melted in our garden here [at the monastery] a
carpet of brown and withered leaves from last fall
was exposed. As we started to rake them away we found
that the earth was covered with young green shoots pushing
up from the earth with an irrepressible energy – the energy
of new life. We have to penetrate beyond the surface to

make contact with the new life of the Resurrection. (PC, p.90)

+━ ━+

In the same way you must regard yourselves as dead to sin and alive to God, in union with Christ Jesus . . . Put yourselves at the disposal of God, as dead men raised to life; yield your bodies to him as implements for doing right; for sin shall no longer be your master, because you are no longer under law, but under the grace of God. (Rom. 6: 11, 13–14)

The gift of his Spirit that is given to each of us is infinite. It is the gift of the totality of God pouring out his Spirit into each of us and our response has to mirror that generosity and totality. It is a call to Christians *not* to respond mindlessly, half-heartedly, occasionally. The call is to respond generously with everything we are, with everything we have at this moment to bring to this response. And we have much to bring. We have our hearts, our minds, our lives, all of which, when we meditate, are integrated, concentrated and aligned on Christ. Everything that we are comes into a harmony with his being, with his love. Nothing is excluded and that is why we have to learn to say the mantra with such total fidelity, total generosity, total attention. The gift *is* given. All we have to do, each of us, is to be open to it, to realise it . . .

. . . Never let anyone discourage you on the path of meditation as in any way being in opposition or conflict with social, political or religious responsibility. The one thing that all societies need is wisdom. There is only one path of wisdom. And the fountainhead of wisdom is to be found in your heart, in the mystery of prayer. (WU, pp.129–30).

+━ ━+

In the same way the Spirit comes to the aid of our weakness. We do not even know how we ought to pray, but through our inarticulate groans the Spirit himself is pleading for us, and God who searches our inmost being knows what the Spirit means . . . (Rom. 8: 26–7)

Now if . . . St Paul and the New Testament as a whole deserve to be taken seriously, we are led to say that prayer is something greater than our talking to God, or imagining God, or imagining holy thoughts. Indeed, as St Paul said, this cannot be a real explanation of prayer if it is true that we do not even know how to pray. But as he goes on to say, 'the Spirit is pleading for us in our inmost being beyond words, beyond thoughts, beyond images, with sighs too deep for words.' (WS, p.39)

+— —+

And those whom he called, he has justified, and to those whom he justified, he has also given his splendour. (Rom. 8: 30)

Meditation is the process in which we take time to allow ourselves to become aware of our infinite potential in the context of the Christ-event . . .
In meditation we open ourselves up to this splendour. Put another way, this means that in meditation we discover both who we are and why we are. In meditation we are not running away from ourselves, we are finding ourselves; we are not rejecting ourselves, we are affirming ourselves. St Augustine put this very succinctly and very beautifully when he said: 'Man must first be restored to himself that, making in himself as it were a stepping-stone, he may rise thence and be borne up to God.' [*Retractions* 1 (viii) 3 (*Migne* PL XXXII)] (WS, p.4)

+— —+

I am convinced that there is nothing in death or in life,
in the realm of spirits or superhuman powers, in the
world as it is or the world as it shall be, in the forces of
the universe, in heights or depths – nothing in all
creation that can separate us from the love of God in
Christ Jesus our Lord. (Rom 8: 38–9)

This is why faithfulness to the daily meditation and to our
mantra during those meditation times is everything. We
know that we must not think about God or imagine God
during these all-important times, simply because he is
present. He is there, not just to be found, but to be loved.
Being in love we let thoughts fall away.

What need then to be discouraged by our distractions?
(WF, p.41).

➤━ ━◄

'The word is near you: it is upon your lips and in your
heart.' This means the word of faith which we proclaim. If on your lips is the confession, 'Jesus is the
Lord', and in your heart the faith that God raised him
from the dead, then you will find salvation. For the
faith that leads to righteousness is in the heart, and the
confession that leads to salvation is upon the lips. (Rom.
10: 8–10)

When St Paul said [this] he [did] not mean that the Christian
is just one who *says* or *thinks* it. If that were all that it
involved then when we stopped thinking 'Jesus is Lord' he
would no longer be Lord for us and we would be merely
part-time pilgrims – which is to say no pilgrim at all,
because a pilgrim is one who stays on the pilgrimage. The
faith St Paul was talking about is a reality that involves our
whole person – that is, a reality that is woven right into the
fabric of our being. We must put on Christ. The Christian

call to transcendence is a call to utter fullness of being. Our faith in the Lord Jesus is a reality present to us whether we are thinking about it or not. (CL, p.91)

The urgency of our day is to find our way back to this pilgrimage [of prayer] and to lead others onto it. Its goal is the person of the Lord Jesus fully alive in our hearts and in the hearts of all people. The means he has chosen for finding him is also personal because when we find ourself we find Jesus. We cannot risk again forgetting that the means are not institutional or structural but personal. The disciple, the teacher, the goal is *personal*. The price and reward is our own personhood. In our end is our beginning. Above all and within all Jesus is Lord, absolutely, personally. (CL, p.33)

+=— —=+

May the God of hope fill you with all joy and peace by your faith in him, until, by the power of the Holy Spirit, you overflow with hope. (Rom. 15: 13)

The discipline of meditation will lead you to a liberty that intoxicates with the joy and peace of the Spirit and sets all your life-experience in the supremely Christian framework of hope . . .

Here is the Christian invitation, therefore, no longer to live at the surface, not to live at the level of glitter and triviality, but to be filled with the peace and with the love of God. In the fullness that ensues you discover your own full reality; discover yourself made real in God. (WU, p.34)

+=— —=+

To him who has power to make your standing sure, according to the Gospel I brought you and the proclamation of Jesus Christ, according to the revelation of that divine secret kept in silence for long ages but now disclosed, and through prophetic scriptures by eternal God's command made known to all nations, to bring them to faith and obedience – to God who alone is wise, through Jesus Christ, be glory for endless ages! Amen. (Rom. 16: 25–7)

The Kingdom *is* established. Faith and obedience teach us to realise it. Remember the practicalities of the work of realisation. Learn to be silent and to love silence. When we meditate we don't look for messages or signs, or phenomena. Each of us must learn to be humble, patient and faithful. Discipline teaches us to be still, and by stillness we learn to empty our heart of everything that is not God, for he requires all the room that our heart has to offer. This emptiness is the purity of heart we develop by saying the mantra with absolute fidelity . . . (HC, p.107)

The First Letter of Saint Paul
to the Corinthians

+>===<+

I thank [God] for all the enrichment that has come to
you in Christ. You possess full knowledge and you can
give full expression to it, because in you the evidence
for the truth of Christ has found confirmation... It is
God himself who called you to share in the life of his
Son Jesus Christ our Lord; and God keeps faith. (1 Cor.
1: 5–6, 9)

Each Christian must once again understand that this is his
and her vocation. Each of us is called to share in the fullness
of the life of Jesus. Christianity is not primarily concerned
with knowledge of God or knowledge about God. It is
concerned with coming to knowledge in God. This sums
up the whole purpose of meditation. Its aim is not to be
thinking of ourselves or to be thinking about God. That is
the last thing we should be doing in meditation. Meditation
is rather the way, the pilgrimage, along which we come to
full knowledge in God. We cannot understand this. We can
only know it in simplicity, in silence and in stillness. (WF,
pp.31–2)

+>===<+

As for me, brothers, when I came to you, I declared the
attested truth of God without display of fine words or
wisdom... I came before you weak... The word I

spoke, the gospel I proclaimed, did not sway you with subtle arguments; it carried conviction by spiritual power, so that your faith might be built not upon human wisdom but upon the power of God. (1 Cor. 2: 1, 3–5)

... Each one of us possesses unknown potential in the extraordinary plan of personal salvation and this is what Jesus discloses to each of us in the stillness of our heart as we undertake the journey of silence and of absolute commitment to silence and pure openness every morning and every evening. What he reveals is that we are created for love, for freedom, for transcendent meaning, for fulfilment; and we realise it all by entering the mystery of the Kingdom that is upon us. That mystery is now unfolded by the generous gift of Christ. (HC, p.106)

＋━ ━＋

For (in the words of Scripture) 'who knows the mind of the Lord? Who can advise him?' We, however, possess the mind of Christ. (1 Cor. 2:16)

As I have said before, if we Christians have a fault, it is that we are so blind to the extraordinary riches that are already ours, achieved for us, given to us by Jesus. We possess the mind of Christ – Christ who knows the Father and who knows us. This is what each of us is invited to discover from our own experience – that we know because we are known and that we love because we are loved ...

That is the invitation given to every one of us so that we may know personally from our own experience all that God of his own grace gives us. The way to that knowledge is

the way of faithfulness, a daily faithfulness to our meditation. (MC, p.56)

The wonder of the Christian revelation is that the consciousness of Christ dwells in our hearts and once we accept that,
then the most important task of our life becomes to be fully
open to it. Our attentiveness to God, our prayer, is eternally
united to the indwelling consciousness of Christ at prayer
within us.

... This is simply what our meditation is about; being
open – wholly, attentively and wakefully – to this great gift
we are given, the human consciousness of Christ alive in
our heart. (HC, pp.14, 15)

The presentness of Christ to us is, as it were, contained
within his presentness in all time. As Christian thinkers
have realised from the beginning, the redemptive love of
Jesus universalised for mankind on the Cross and occu-
pying the centre of all consciousness through the
Resurrection, travels both backwards and forwards through
space and time, uniting every human consciousness in him.
From this moment, in and out of time, man has been
plunged into a radically new way of being within the
mystery of God. He has been touched by a ray of reality
that has opened his eyes to the ambiance within which he
lives and moves and has his being. He is now empowered to
be with God in a quite unprecedented way, by participating
directly and wholly in the plenitude of God's Being ...
(PC, p.51)

The ongoing pilgrimage of meditation leads us to an ever-
deepening encounter with the essential theology of prayer.
What does St Paul mean when he says we possess the mind
of Christ? We know from the doctrine of the indwelling of
the Holy Spirit that the fullness of God is to be found in
our own hearts. We know that the full life of the Trinity is

lived in our hearts. This is because Jesus Christ dwells in
our hearts. His human consciousness is to be found within
each of us. The journey of prayer is simply to find the
way to open our human consciousness to his human consciousness, and to become, on that way, fully conscious
ourselves . . .

The way of meditation is the way of opening ourselves
as fully as possible in this life to the gift of God. His gift,
par excellence, is Jesus Christ. He is our light. He is our
enlightenment . . . (WU, p.60)

Surely you know that you are God's temple, where the
Spirit of God dwells. (1 Cor. 3: 16)

Each of us is invited to that self-knowledge for ourselves.
It is not enough to know it in somebody else's witness; we
must know it through the living word of God as it dwells
in our hearts. But we do not know this through our own
power; we know it through his self-revealing power. It is
this power that is revealed in us when we become silent
and attentive. (WU, p.121)

Make no mistake about this: if there is anyone among
you who fancies himself wise – wise, I mean, by the
standards of this passing age – he must become a fool
to gain true wisdom. (1 Cor. 3: 18)

The way of meditation seems to the world foolish. That we
do leave behind thoughts, images and words because of
our faith in this reality of Christ is foolishness of
divine wisdom. We leave behind limited, finite thoughts
and words to be open to the unlimited love of God in

Jesus. The absoluteness of God's gift makes fools of us all . . .

Saying the mantra, morning and evening, every day of our life is a way of foolishness in the eyes of the world. But it leads to the only wisdom there is: full consciousness in the consciousness of Jesus. (HC, p.78)

+— —+

Make no mistake about this: if there is anyone among you who fancies himself wise – wise, I mean, by the standards of this passing age – he must become a fool to gain true wisdom. For the wisdom of this world is folly in God's sight. (1 Cor. 3: 18–19)

The cloud of this unknowing is the cloud by which the presence of God as well as the inner nature of his hiddenness is so often described in the Bible. A cloud that both leads us through the desert (Exodus 13: 22) and draws us into itself to speak the Word (Luke 9: 35) – the cloud, too, in which we have only to say our little word (*The Cloud of Unknowing*, Chap.7). (LH, p.83)

+— —+

Do you not know that your body is a shrine of the indwelling Holy Spirit, and the Spirit is God's gift to you? (1 Cor. 6: 19)

The diffusion of our essential harmony throughout our being is another way of saying that the prayer of the spirit of Jesus wells up in our hearts, floods our hearts and overflows throughout us. This is the amazing gift we have been given by Jesus sending us His Spirit. But He does not force it on us. It is for us to recognise it and accept it, and this we do, not by being clever or self-analytical, but by being silent, by being simple. The gift is already given. We have merely to open our hearts to its infinite generosity. The mantra opens our hearts in pure simplicity . . . (WS, p.73)

+— —+

Am I not an apostle? Did I not see Jesus our Lord? (1 Cor. 9: 1)

Neither Paul nor Luke had known the historical Jesus. But what they are both proclaiming is the profound Christian reality that the 'Way' is not merely a historical tradition but is something much greater: our own lived experience of the present reality of the risen Lord Jesus, the Christ. (LH, pp.46–7)

+— —+

All these things that happened to them were symbolic and were recorded for our benefit as a warning. For upon us the fulfilment of the ages has come. (1 Cor. 10: 11)

The faith of the Christic consciousness contains this extra-ordinary sense of having reached the fullness of time. When it is repeated as a mere theological formula it inevitably sounds astonishingly arrogant. But spoken out of the experience of the Spirit who inspired the prophets to imagine such a time it becomes mysteriously persuasive and strangely non-controversial . . .

To hear this proclaimed with authority is to be awakened to an unexpected experience – not merely to the presentness of Christ in time and in our own lifetime but also to the fraternity of all mankind that this creates. We recognise our solidarity as men because we stand together, in the same place and in the same time before the same mystery . . . (PC, p.55)

✦ ✦

In a word, there are three things that last forever: faith, hope, and love; but the greatest of them all is love. (1 Cor. 13: 13)

The truly religious understanding of man is not found in terms of reward and punishment, but in terms of wholeness and division. The supreme religious insight in East and West is that all our alienations are resolved, and all our thinking and feeling powers united, in the heart . . .

The holy men of the Orthodox Church see the essential task of the Christian life as being to restore this unity to man with a mind and heart integrated through prayer. The mantra provides this integrating power. It is like a harmonic that we sound in the depths of our spirit, bringing us to an ever-deepening sense of our own wholeness and central harmony. It leads us to the source of this harmony, to our centre, rather as a radar bleep leads an aircraft home through thick fog. It also rearranges us, in the sense that it brings all our powers and faculties into line with each other just as a magnet drawn over iron filings pulls them into their proper force fields. (WS, p.15)

✦ ✦

. . . and when all things are thus subject to him, then the Son himself will also be made subordinate to God who made all things subject to him, and thus God will be all in all. (1 Cor. 15: 28)

The inner journey is a way of union. Firstly, it unites

us to ourselves. Then (as our personal fulfilment is found beyond ourselves) it unites us to others. And then (as union with others opens up the heart of the mystery of love to us) it unites us with God, so that God may be all in all. (DJ, p.2)

The Second Letter of Saint Paul
to the Corinthians

+╼━ ━╾+

The Son of God, Christ Jesus, proclaimed among you by us ... was never a blend of Yes and No. With him it was, and is, Yes. He is the Yes pronounced upon God's promises, every one of them. That is why, when we give glory to God, it is through Jesus Christ that we say 'Amen'. And if you and we belong to Christ, guaranteed as his and anointed, it is all God's doing; it is God also who has set his seal upon us, and as a pledge of what is to come has given the Spirit to dwell in our hearts. (2 Cor. 1: 19–22)

The way of meditation is only the way of love: 'this work of love,' as *The Cloud of Unknowing* calls it. And so it is real, not theoretical; incarnate, not abstract; practical, not just a matter of words or ideas. To act upon this vision and really to begin the journey requires a decisive and open commitment. There is, though, no commitment without the simplicity of spirit that allows us to say an unambiguous 'yes' to the invitation to journey to reality. The danger of this, of course, is that it sounds like – and can lead us into – the worst form of self-centred self-importance ... until we understand that the 'yes' we utter is Christ himself. (LH, p.81)

Meditation is a practice that enables us each day to root our lives in the spiritual reality of God. It is a positive way, even though our current materialistic and outer-directed values may dismiss it as a waste of time or as unproductive introversion. Yet in meditation we do not reject the world or construct any false opposition to it. We wish to live fully in the world but we know we can only arrive at that fullness and wholeheartedness if we are truly rooted in God. (WF, p.56)

＋━   ━＋

Where the Spirit of the Lord is, there is liberty. (2 Cor. 3: 17)

Saying the mantra is a discipline which helps us to transcend all the limitations of our narrow and isolated self-obsession. The mantra leads us into an experience of the liberty that reigns at the centre of our being . . . It introduces us to this liberty by helping us to pass over into the Other, by helping us to take our minds off ourselves. This is what Jesus means by leaving self behind. (WS, p.58)

＋━   ━＋

For the same God who said, 'Out of darkness let light shine', has caused his light to shine within us, to give the light of revelation – the revelation of the glory of God in the face of Jesus Christ. (2 Cor. 4: 6)

The power of this light is to be found within our own hearts, within each one of us. What we each must learn to do is to be open to that power and to live our lives out of it. What I suggest to you is that you try to build into the structure of your life a time each morning and evening to be still, to be silent, to be humble, to be simple, to *be* in God. (MC, pp.3–4)

Christ is light. He is the light that gives range and depth to our vision. He is also, in his fully realised human consciousness, the eyes with which we see the Father in the divine perspective. Without his light our vision would be tied to the partial dimension and our spirit could not soar above itself into the infinite liberty and crystal clarity of the unified state. Our consciousness would, however wonderful, remain an observer on the periphery of his space, unfulfilled by union with his consciousness, unco-ordinated with his Body. Without his Spirit dwelling in our mortal bodies and opening up the infinite dimension within our spirit, we would be like men restricted by their own innate limitations from moving freely in the liberty they have been given. But the light that transforms our weakness, that makes our limitations the crucible in which his power is brought to perfection, has been freely given, poured into our heart as the pure effulgence of the Father, for Christ is the radiance of the Father. The light we need to empower our vision is not less than this radiance, the glory of God itself . . .

For those of us humbly treading the pilgrimage of prayer into this experience of light this is the only fundamental knowledge we need . . . (PC, pp.15, 16)

＋━ ━＋

No wonder we do not lose heart! Though our outward humanity is in decay, yet day by day we are inwardly renewed. Our troubles are slight and short-lived; and their outcome an eternal glory which outweighs them far. Meanwhile our eyes are fixed, not on the things that are seen, but on the things that are unseen: for what is seen passes away; what is unseen is eternal . . . We groan indeed, we who are enclosed within this earthly frame; we are oppressed because we do not want to have the old body stripped off. Rather our desire is to have the new body put on over it, so that our mortal part may

be absorbed in life immortal. God himself has shaped us
for this very end; and as a pledge of it he has given
us the Spirit. Therefore we never cease to be confident.
(2 Cor. 4: 16—5: 6)

Within the structure of our daily life, this inward renewal
of which St Paul speaks is the purpose and fruit of our
twice-daily meditation. We are literally made new in the
fact of entering into the ever-deeper centres of being, and
of knowing ever more fully the harmony of all our qualities
and energies in that ultimate centre of our being which is
the centre and source of all being, the centre of the Trinita-
rian love . . . (WS, pp.32–3)

The vision of the *unseen* and the confidence that comes from
being absorbed in the *immortal* is what meditation is about.
We know with an unshakable conviction when we die to
self that what we stand on, that is eternal. This is to know
that our being may pass through stage to stage of life,
through many deaths, but we can never slip out of *being*.
God never withdraws the gift he has given and to have
given us our being is to have made it immortal. That is the
essential preparation we need *in experience* to face our own
death without fear, without false consolation, with open
minds and open hearts. (DJ, pp.8–9)

Our gift of spiritual knowledge, our capacity to know by
participation, is our gift of life. Whatever our experience
may be, it recalls us to the grounding realisation that we
are and, in contacting this ground of our being – the consciousness that we simply are – we are filled with joy: and
the consciousness that Being is Joy once more transforms the
pattern of our experience . . . Each time we meditate we
return to this grounding consciousness of Being, and each
time we return to the changing pattern of our life more
firmly rooted in our being and so more able to perceive life

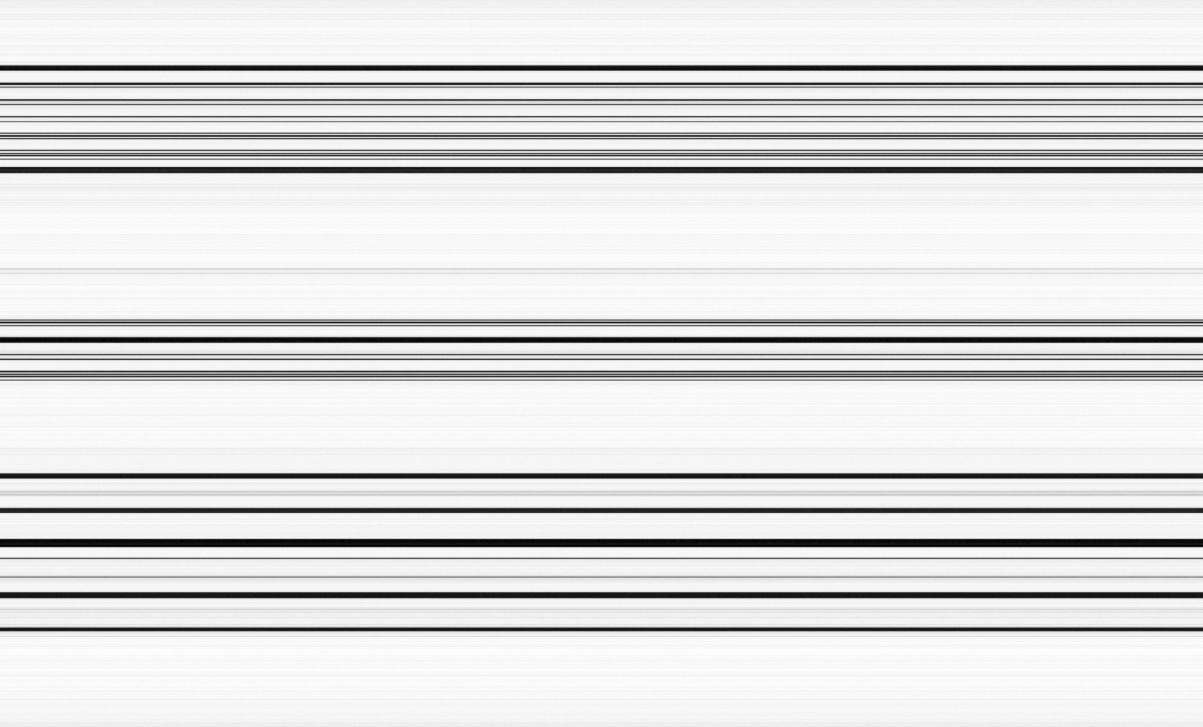

. . . Meditating,

to dominate. We

being the person

is as a result of th

and with the po

to be and the en

impossible to be

requires of us gr

to let go of our

fears and anxie

meditation so th

selves at all tim

see who God is a

this, we are in l

When anyon

'a new creati

has already b

The relevance

ourselves is tha

rejecting experi

deeper significa

seen to be interp

love. (CL, p.15)

Remember: s

fully, and yo

There is a marv

But the call to t

for real genero

as mystery and to communicate this perception in joy to others. Our ability to see this is itself the gift of our creation – the gift that is being given with ever-increasing generosity moment by moment. Our creation is ever expanding in harmony with the overflowing love occurring in the secret depths of the Father's timeless mystery. As his being fills our being, our heart is purified and we are led deeper into the vision of God that is his own infinitely generous self-knowledge. (PC, pp.14–15)

━ ━

Our mortal part may be absorbed into life immortal. (2 Cor. 5: 4)

In the Christian vision of eternal life – which means full realisation of all potentiality – nothing is rejected or wasted. Even our most fragile and ephemeral dimension, our body, is to be 'saved' from the entropic processes that so frighten us . . . (PC, p.91)

━ ━

For the love of Christ leaves us no choice, when once we have reached the conclusion that one man died for all and therefore all mankind has died. His purpose in dying for all was that men, while still in life, should cease to live for themselves, and should live for him who for their sake died and was raised to life. With us therefore worldly standards have ceased to count in our estimate of any man; even if once they counted in our understanding of Christ, they do so now no longer. When anyone is united to Christ, there is a new world; the old order has gone, and a new order has already begun. (2 Cor. 5: 14–17)

... Meditating, we let go of the desire to control, to possess, to dominate. We seek instead only to be *who we are* and being the person we are, we are open to the God who is. It is as a result of that openness that we are filled with wonder and with the power and energy of God which is the power to be and the energy to be *in love*. When we are in love it is impossible to be bored ... Entering into this state however requires of us great generosity, the largeness and confidence to let go of our plans, of our hopes, as well as of our fears and anxieties. We begin by doing this at the time of meditation so that we may be detached enough to be ourselves at all times, free enough to see beyond ourselves, to see who God is and who the person with us truly is. Seeing this, we are in love always. (HC, pp.44–5)

When anyone is united to Christ, there is a new world 'a new creation'; the old order has gone, and a new order has already begun. (2 Cor. 5: 17)

The relevance of this witness of the early Christians for ourselves is that it was not an other-worldly or world-rejecting experience. It was much more an experience of the deeper significance of the whole of creation which was now seen to be interpenetrated with the power of Christ's saving love. (CL, p.15)

Remember: sparse sowing, sparse reaping; sow bountifully, and you will reap bountifully. (2 Cor. 9: 6)

There is a marvellous harvest for all of us in our own spirit. But the call to this openness to the spirit of Jesus does ask for real generosity from each of us. Firstly we need generosity in putting aside the half-hour for meditation every morning and every evening. And I understand very well that that does ask for a very generous response and a very creative response, given the tasks and responsibilities of your own lives. Secondly, a great generosity is called for in the actual time of your meditation to say your word, *maranatha*, from the beginning to the end. So often we want to follow our own thoughts, our own insights, our own religious feeling. But we must learn to leave everything behind and to seek the spirit in our own hearts. (MC, p.6)

The Letter of Saint Paul
to the Galatians

+⇥— ⇤+

I have been crucified with Christ: the life I now live is
not my life, but the life which Christ lives in me; and
my present bodily life is lived by faith in the Son of God,
who loved me and gave himself up for me. (Gal. 2: 20)

Meditation is the journey beyond our existence to our being.
To our own unique being. It is the journey to the essential
core of what and who we are. The wonderful thing we
know in the Christian revelation is that, even more than
that, it is the journey into the heart of Being itself. It is the
journey into God. The one who made us *who* we are . . . We
must set out on this journey for ourselves if we are to see,
in the light of the Christian gospel, that the journey is
beyond ourselves into absolute and essential being. Being
who is God, the God who is Love. (WU, pp.24–5)

+⇥— ⇤+

For through faith you are all children of God in union
with Christ Jesus. Baptised into union with him, you
have all put on Christ as a garment. There is no such
thing as Jew and Greek, slave and free man, male and
female; for you are all one person in Christ Jesus. (Gal.
3: 26–8)

In meditation, and in the life enriched by meditation, we

just are fully ourselves, whoever we are. That is why meditation is a school of community because in discovering our own oneness, our own being and potential, we are aware that others possess being, potential, and their unique value is what leads us to service. So, meditation is a good school of community because by it we learn both to communicate and serve. The ultimate end of meditation is communion. Not only do we discover our own oneness but we discover our oneness with *the All* and with all. The path is a path of simplicity achieved through the practice of silence. In the deep silence that each of us must discover in our own hearts, mystery is revealed and it is revealed simply because we pay attention to it.

In meditation we know because we are known. This spiritual knowledge is the basis of community and the universal Christ...

As we meditate, we put aside all division and dividedness and we cross the divide of alienation, the divide of division, and we seek to be one with God. We find we *are* one with God. (WU, pp.19–20)

The Letter of Saint Paul to the Ephesians

✝── ──✝

> Therein lies the richness of God's free grace lavished upon us, imparting full wisdom and insight. He has made known to us his hidden purpose – such was his will and pleasure determined beforehand in Christ – to be put into effect when the time was ripe: namely, that the universe, all in heaven and all on earth, might be brought into a unity in Christ. (Eph. 1: 8–10)

That sounds inspiring when you listen to it but it is only words, verbal inspiration, unless you enter into the experience of it – unless you enter into a way of prayer, the meditation that can leave analysis behind and open your heart and mind to the great synthesis that happens in Christ, with Christ and through Christ. (MC, p.40)

Everyone who perseveres in meditation discovers that although during our time of meditation it might appear that nothing happens, yet gradually the whole of our life is changed. We have to be patient because we might like it to be changed more rapidly. Our thought gradually becomes clarified, relationships become more loving, and this is because, in the process of meditation, we are made free to love *by* Love. The reason for all this is really very simple. When we meditate, not only do we stand back from the individual operations of our being, but we begin to learn to find a wholly new ground to stand on. We discover a rootedness of being which is not just in ourselves, but we discover ourselves rooted in God. Rooted in God who is Love. (WU, p.11)

+— —+

I pray that the God of our Lord Jesus Christ, the all-glorious Father, may give you the spiritual powers of wisdom and vision, by which there comes the knowledge of him. I pray that your inward eyes may be illumined so that you may know what is the hope to which he calls you, what the wealth and glory of the share he offers you . . . and how vast the resources of his power open to us who trust in him. They are measured by his strength and the might which he exerted in Christ when he raised him from the dead. (Eph. 1: 17–20)

Meditation is the way that is entirely open to God because it is open to our own being and to the whole of creation. The Way is a free flowing way and it flows with the power of God that we discover in the depths of our own being. In that power, with that power and through that power we come to meet God in creation. So what is there that is passive about meditation? Meditation is learning to live out of the fullness of power. That power is the life of God and it is the power of Love. (WU, p.119)

+— —+

I pray that your inward eyes may be illumined, so that you may know what is the hope to which he calls you, what the wealth and glory of the share he offers you . . . and how vast the resources of his power open to us who trust in him. (Eph. 1: 18–19)

For our lives to be fully human we need to encounter the

Spirit of love within ourselves. It is not a journey just for spiritual experts. It is a journey for everyone who would live their lives to the full . . .

Meditation is the great way of trust. We sit down, we sit still, we say our mantra with growing fidelity and trust our whole selves utterly to God. We do that every morning and every evening of our lives and thus we learn to live out of the trust, to live out of the love that faith reveals and liberates. (HC, pp.100, 101)

+=—   —=+

So he came and proclaimed the good news; peace to you who were far off and peace to those who were nearby; for through him, we both alike have access to the Father in the one Spirit. (Eph. 2: 17)

That is what meditation is about – access to the Father in the one Spirit, the Spirit who dwells in your heart and in mine, the Spirit who is the Spirit of God. Christian meditation is simply openness to that Spirit, in the depth of our being, in all simplicity, in all humility, in all love. (MC, p.22)

+=—   —=+

With this is mind, then, I kneel in prayer to the Father, from whom every family in heaven and on earth takes its name, that out of the treasures of his glory he may grant you strength and power through his Spirit in your inner being, that through faith Christ may dwell in your hearts in love. With deep roots and firm foundations, may you be strong to grasp, with all God's people, what is the breadth and length and height and depth of the love of Christ, and to know it, though it is beyond knowledge. So may you attain to fullness of being, the fullness of God himself. (Eph. 3: 14–19)

This is a marvellously comprehensive description of the destiny that each of us has, as Christians, as human beings. Our destiny and call is to come to a fullness of being which is the fullness of God himself. In other words, each of us is summoned to an unlimited, infinite development through the way of faith and love, as we leave the narrowness of our own ego behind, and enter into the ever-expanding mystery of God's own self.

. . . Jesus has told us that his Spirit is to be found in our hearts. Meditating is uncovering this truth as a present reality deep within ourselves at the centre of our lives. The Spirit that we are invited to discover in our heart is the power source that enriches every aspect and part of our life. The Spirit is the eternal Spirit of life and the almighty Spirit of love. (HC, p.98)

. . . Learning to say your mantra, leaving behind all other words, ideas, imaginations and fantasies, is learning to enter into the presence of the Spirit who dwells in your inner heart, who dwells there in love. The Spirit of God dwells in our hearts in silence, and it is in humility and in faith that we must enter into that silent presence. (MC, p.75)

+►═ ═◄+

With deep roots and firm foundations, may you be strong to grasp, with all God's people, what is the breadth and length and height and depth of the love of Christ, and to know it, though it is beyond knowledge. (Eph. 3: 18)

We have to prepare our hearts to receive the wonderful message of the Gospel in all its fullness. And until we have expanded our consciousness, we will be incapable of taking in anything of the grand scale of the message of our redemption, and we will be incapable too of knowing what the traditional religious language we use really means. Until an expansion of our consciousness takes place our minds and hearts will be too limited, too absorbed in day-to-day trivia. Meditation is precisely the way we need to follow in order to expand our hearts, broaden our vision and, as Blake said, 'cleanse the doors of perception'. (WS, p.17)

+= =+

So shall we all at last attain to the unity inherent in our faith and our knowledge of the Son of God – to mature manhood, measured by nothing less than the full stature of Christ. (Eph. 4: 13)

Meditation is so important for us because it is a way of actual response that leads us away from self. It is a way of transcendence. It is a way of entering the reality that is greater than ourselves. It is a way that brings us into that liberty of spirit that arises when we are no longer thinking about ourselves, our plans, our self-development and our fulfilment. While meditating we have only one consider-ation, which is to enter into a state of harmonious resonance with the divinising energy of God. In the Christian vision the energy of God is limitless, free, self-communicating love. In the Christian revelation, this is the call that each of us has, to allow that love to become *the* supreme reality in our lives. (HC, pp.68–9)

+= =+

Let us speak the truth in love; so shall we fully grow up into Christ. (Eph. 4: 15)

To know that this transcendent mystery is humanly rooted in our daily lives and our loving relationships with each other is the great source of Christian joy – and the great power of the Christian presence in the world. What Saint Benedict says of monks in the last chapter of the Rule expresses the generosity of the universal Christian family that finds its unity and vitality in the presence of Jesus: 'Let them put absolutely nothing before Christ and may he bring us all together to life eternal.' (LH, p.76)

+━ ━+

'Awake, sleeper, rise from the dead,
And Christ will shine upon you.' (Eph. 5: 14)

To awaken is to open our eyes, and we open them, as St Benedict said, 'to the divinising light'. What we see transforms what we are.

Each time we meditate we take a step further into this wakefulness, this state of being in light. And the more fully we integrate the basic Christian experience into our ordinary daily life the more deeply wakeful we become. This makes our life a journey of discovery, an exploration, a constantly renewed miracle of created vitality. To meditate is to put an end to dullness, to fear, and above all to pettiness ... The man who is awake knows without doubt he is awake. But the man who is dreaming also believes he is awake. In that state, the images of a dream convince us that they are the realities we know as real when we are awake. We enter wakefulness, as the meditator knows, by letting go of the images and by learning to wait for the Reality – for 'Christ to shine upon you'. (PC, pp.73, 74)

+━ ━+

Be most careful then how you conduct yourselves: like sensible men, not like simpletons. Use the present opportunity to the full, for these are evil days. So do not be fools, but try to understand what the will of the Lord is.

> Do not give way to drunkenness and the dissipation that
> goes with it, but let the Holy Spirit fill you: speak to one
> another in psalms, hymns and songs; sing and make
> music in your hearts to the Lord; and in the name of our
> Lord Jesus Christ give thanks every day for everything
> to our God and Father. (Eph. 5: 15–20)

We need to be more conscious of the destiny that is given
to us by God, and more courageous in responding to it . . .

Let me remind you again of the necessity for faithfulness,
in particular for the daily faithfulness to your meditation,
what ever the difficulties (and they are often considerable);
and your faithfulness, too, during the time of meditation
to the recitation of the mantra. It is this simplicity, this
faithfulness, that leads us directly into the fullness of the
mystery which is the mystery of our own destiny, the
mystery of the self-revelation of God and the mystery of
the love of God in Jesus . . . (HC, pp.71, 72)

The Letter of Saint Paul
to the Philippians

┼═══ ═══┼

> All I care for is to know Christ, to experience the power of his resurrection, and to share his sufferings, in growing conformity with his death, if only I may finally arrive at the resurrection from the dead . . . He will transfigure the body belonging to our humble state, and give it a form like that of his own resplendent body, by the very power which enables him to make all things subject to himself. Therefore, my friends, beloved friends whom I long for, my joy, my crown, stand thus firm in the Lord. (Phil. 3: 10–11, 21–4: 1)

One thing we learn in meditation is the priority of being over action. Indeed, no action has any meaning, or at least any lasting depth of meaning, unless it springs from being, from the depths of your own being. That is why meditation is a way that leads us away from shallowness to depth, to profundity. Learning to be is learning to begin to live out of the fullness of life. That is the invitation. It is learning to begin to be a full person. The mysterious thing about the Christian revelation is that as we live our lives fully, we live out the eternal consequences of our own creation. We are no longer living as if we were exhausting a limited supply of life that we received at our birth. What we know from the teaching of Jesus is that we become infinitely filled with life when we are at one with the source of our being and enter fully into union with our Creator, the One who *is*, a God who describes himself as 'I Am'. (MC, pp.10–11, 12)

+━ ━+

The peace of God, which is beyond our utmost understanding, will keep guard over your hearts and your
thoughts, in Christ Jesus. (Phil. 4: 7)

What we have to learn is to seek that peace absolutely.
Some people would think that it is unwise to speak of the
absolute commitment that Jesus calls us to. Some people
would think that even to hear about it is only for experts.
But as far as I can understand it, the invitation of Jesus is
given to each of us to take up our cross, to follow him to
Calvary and to join him and to go through with him, into
the infinite love of the Father. (MC, pp.114)

The Letter of Saint Paul
to the Colossians

+>= =<+

We ask God that you may receive from him all wisdom and spiritual understanding for full insight into his will, so that your manner of life may be worthy of the Lord and entirely pleasing to him. We pray that you may bear fruit in active goodness of every kind, and grow in the knowledge of God. May he strengthen you, in his glorious might, with ample power to meet whatever comes with fortitude, patience, and joy; and to give thanks to the Father who has made you fit to share the heritage of God's people in the realm of light. (Col. 1: 9–12)

... The way of meditation is at the same time the way of compassion, of simplicity and of joy. Only one thing is necessary for us to follow this way and that is to tread the pilgrimage with utter seriousness, not half-heartedly but whole-heartedly and single-mindedly. The Christian mystery has always called us to this wholeness and perfect sincerity, where our poverty leads to the riches of the Kingdom and a life lived in active goodness of every kind. (HC, p.61)

+>= =<+

May he strengthen you, in his glorious might, with ample power to meet whatever comes with fortitude, patience and joy; and to give thanks to the Father who

> has made you fit to share the heritage of God's people
> in the realm of light. (Col. 1: 11–12)

There is nothing passive whatsoever about meditation. It is
a state of growing and deepening openness with the power
source of all reality which we can only adequately describe
in words as God-who-is-love. The aim of our life and the
invitation of our life is nothing less than complete union,
full resonance with that power source . . .

Meditation is about openness to that 'ample power' of
God. (MC, p.50)

⊢━ ━⊣

> In him everything in heaven and on earth was created,
> not only things visible but also the invisible orders . . .
> the whole universe has been created through him and
> for him. (Col. 1: 16)

In the experience of meditation we discover a growing
awareness of unity. The mantra, as I have said before, is
like a harmonic that sounds within and brings us into
a harmonious unity with the whole of creation, within
and without. It is like – I am talking poetically – the
harmonic of God bringing us into harmony and union
with God himself. This experience of unity inspired St
Paul's vision of the cosmic Christ filling the whole
universe and leaving no part of it untouched by his redemptive love.

Through the experience of meditation we come to understand that each of us, meaning every living human being,
is in a creative relationship with God through Christ. (WF,
p.16)

⊢━ ━⊣

> The secret is this: Christ in you, the hope of a glory to come. He it is whom we proclaim. (Col. 1: 27–8)

> He rescued us from the domain of darkness and brought us away into the kingdom of his dear Son, in whom our release is secured and our sins forgiven. (Col. 1: 13–15)

God has given us himself. Nothing has been kept back. He has given us the fullness of the divinity in the humanity of Jesus. A Christian life is our response to that gift and, just as the gift is absolute, so must our response be absolute and permanent. In responding to the gift of God in meditation we place ourselves wholly at his disposition. We do not even think any of our own thoughts. We do not even tell God of our own thoughts. We are simply and totally at his disposition by responding totally to the gift, body and mind, in absolute silence. (HC, p.7)

⊷ ⊶

> Therefore, since Jesus was delivered to you as Christ and Lord, live your lives in union with him. Be rooted in him; be built in him; be consolidated in the faith you were taught; let your hearts overflow with thankfulness ... For it is in Christ that the complete being of the Godhead dwells embodied, and in him you have been brought to completion. (Col. 2: 6–7, 9)

The one thing we must understand is that in the time of meditation we need not think about anything. This is the time of the day for total attention, for total openness, for total love. The Christian experience is, in essence, a certain knowledge that God is love and that he lives in our hearts. Our call, therefore, is more than to dialogue with him, it is to be in union with him. To be one with him, each of us must come to the fullness of our own created oneness. Each of us must experience our own harmony in order that we may be in total harmony with him. The Christian way is a way where each of us is made whole by becoming completely stable, completely rooted in truth, in love, in goodness, in justice. In fact, in God.

Meditation is simply the time for realising that rootedness . . . (HC, pp.86–7)

+— —+

Did you not die with Christ and pass beyond reach of the elemental spirits of the universe? Then why behave as though you were still living the life of the world? Why let people dictate to you? . . . Were you not raised to life in Christ? Then aspire to the realm above, where Christ is, seated at the right hand of God, and let your thoughts dwell on that higher realm, not on this earthly life. I repeat, you died; and now your life lies hidden with Christ in God. When Christ, who is our life, is manifested, then you too will be manifested with him in glory. (Col. 2: 20, 3: 1–4)

Strictly speaking, meditation does not give us any experience of God. God does not 'experience' himself but rather he *knows*. For him to experience himself would suggest a divided consciousness. What meditation does is to take us into the life of God, the life full of knowledge of the Word begotten from self-transcendence. This is why meditation is an entry into divinisation through Jesus. Through him we become one with God. With him we utterly transcend ourselves, leaving the whole of ourselves behind and becoming a new creation in him. In him, meditation is itself the process of self-transcendence. (HC, p.17)

+— —+

Whatever you are doing, put your whole heart into it, as if you were doing it for the Lord and not for men, knowing that there is a Master who will give you your heritage as a reward for your service. (Col. 3: 23–4)

Put your whole heart into it. Meditation calls us to the deepest and clearest level of understanding. Once we begin to meditate, once we have taken the first step, we soon realise that we can no longer remain in the shallows. The call we have responded to is for a complete reorientation of our being, a radical conversion. The call is, above all else, to enter the mystery itself, to learn what cannot be learned anywhere else or in any other way ... God, our Creator and our Father, calls us to an intimacy with him that arises because God first knows and loves us. And, in this act of knowing and loving us, God invites us to come into a relationship of knowing and loving him. (WU, p.97)

The Second Letter of Saint Paul
to the Thessalonians

✦✦ ✦✦

We are bound to thank God always for you, brothers
beloved by the Lord, because from the beginning of
time God chose you to find salvation in the Spirit that
consecrates you, and in the truth that you believe. It was
for this that he called you through the gospel which we
brought, so that you might possess for your own the
splendour of our Lord Jesus Christ. (2 Thess. 2: 13–14)

Those words give us some idea of what the invitation is –
salvation in the Spirit. Salvation in the Spirit means being
taken utterly beyond ourselves into supreme liberty of
being in the Spirit of God. We are called to that now. 'The
kingdom of heaven is among you.' We are called to it in
the most practical way – to take our day and to put eternal
life in the first place of our day. It is in eternal life that we
turn definitively from death and dying. The only ultimate
tragedy is a life that has not opened to eternal life. The only
ultimate tragedy is a life that is dying (MC, p.67)

✦✦ ✦✦

May the Lord direct your hearts towards God's love and
the steadfastness of Christ! (2 Thess. 3: 5)

... The way of meditation is a way of knowing reality
simply because it is only by this most complete and undif-

ferentiated union with the Creator that we can live fully out of our own roots. To live fully is to be conscious of our origin and so live fully out of the power of God. For this awareness we need to be steadfast. We need that steel in the spine that will enable us to return day after day to meditation; not concerned so much with progress or enlightenment or success but with the faithful, humble return to our task. In meditation as Christians our hearts are directed towards God's love. Each of us has to discover and then to remember, knowing it with absolute clarity and certainty, that we are infinitely loveable and infinitely loved. We must know it, not just as an intellectual proposition but with experiential knowledge, in our own hearts. It is the most important knowledge there is for any of us and that is why meditation is so important. By meditating we can fasten our minds and hearts upon the essential fact of history, the pivotal knowledge of the human mind, that God is love. (HC, p.103)

The First Letter of Saint Paul
to Timothy

+⊨ ⊨+

Religion does yield high dividends, but only to the man whose resources are within him. (1 Tim. 6: 6)

The interiority of these resources of the eternal reality constitute the spiritual nature of the journey of meditation. But they are interior not introspective. Anyone who meditates in faith knows that the journey within takes us out of ourselves. The deeper we penetrate within the more we make contact with others and with the multiplicity and variety of creation. And yet the more wonderfully we see it all in unity – a unity whose centre lies within ourselves ... (DJ, p.8)

The Letter
to the Hebrews

✦— —✦

Let us then stop discussing the rudiments of Christianity.
We ought not to be laying over again the foundations of
faith in God ... Let us advance towards maturity; and
so we shall, if God permits. (Heb. 6: 1, 3)

One can be quite sincere living off the ideas and images of
our faith but, as our ordinary experience is constantly reminding us, sincerity alone is not ultimately satisfying. Our call
as Christians is a call beyond thought and image and sincerity to that essential encounter with Reality, the encounter
with Reality itself, and it is this encounter which makes us
authentic. We are not only called, but we are empowered to
respond, because of the unique and fundamental transform-
ation of our consciousness that has occurred as a result of
the life of Jesus. The consciousness of a fully human being
has opened in love to the infinite mystery of God. It has
been swept out of itself into God but without ceasing to
be itself. The mystery of the Incarnation means that Jesus
remains fully human, fully alive to us and to the Father in
his glorified state. And so it is through his human consciousness that we can make that same journey into authenticity:
our call is to be realised by being bathed in the light of that
reality, the reality that has glorified him ... (PC, p.71)

✦— —✦

When men have once been enlightened, when they have
had a taste of the heavenly gift . . . and after all this
have fallen away, it is impossible to bring them again to
repentance. (Heb. 6: 4, 6)

It is not that God withdraws his gift, as it were in pique; I
think what the writer of the Letter to the Hebrews means
is that, if we persist in treating ourselves trivially, we can
mortally damage our capacity to receive the divine gift. The
call to meditate every day of our lives is simply the call to
take the words of Jesus seriously. We take them seriously
by turning to his presence in our hearts every morning and
every evening of our lives as our first responsibility. (PC,
p.76)

+= =+

But now Christ has come, high priest of the good things
already in being. The tent of his priesthood is a greater
and more perfect one, not made by men's hands, that is,
not belonging to this created world; the blood of his
sacrifice is his own blood . . . and thus he has entered
the sanctuary once and for all and secured an eternal
deliverance . . . How much greater is the power of the
blood of Christ; he offered himself without blemish to
God, a spiritual and eternal sacrifice; and his blood will
cleanse our conscience from the deadness of our former
ways and will fit us for the service of the living God.
(Heb. 9: 11–14)

. . . What we have to discover in meditation, and what each
of us, I think, *must* discover if we are to live our lives to
the full, is that the reality of God is the only foundation we
can build on. Any thought of God, any emotion concerning
God is subject to the shifting sands of our impermanent
levels of consciousness. Meditation is the awakening to the

reality of God at that level in ourselves where we do not have a shrine-image of him or a cult-devotion to him, but where God is, in his pure and gracious self-giving. This presence is the only ultimate sanity because God is the only ultimate reality. In God alone can we find the courage to see what is to be seen, to travel the road we must travel. In God alone can we find the strength to take up our cross. And in God alone can we find that cross to be a burden sweet and light. (WU, p.104)

+━ ━+

So now, my friends, the blood of Jesus makes us free to enter boldly into the sanctuary by the new, living way which he has opened for us through the curtain, the way of his flesh. (Heb. 10: 19–20)

One of the biggest religious problems that we face is really allowing God to be free. So often we want to control him, getting him to see everything from our point of view and to make things turn out as we would want them to. But setting the mantra free in your heart is a preparation, indeed a sacrament, for allowing God to be totally free in your heart, at the centre of your life.

. . . People often say to me, 'Isn't this way of meditation a way of ignoring the humanity of Christ?' If only we can learn to say our mantra we will discover the fullness of that humanity, the fullness of Christ's love, close to us, present to us, in our hearts. (HC, pp.31, 32, 33)

+━ ━+

Faith gives substance to our hopes, and makes us certain of realities we do not see. (Heb. 11: 1)

The influence of the scientific method on our entire way of responding to life has persuaded us not to believe in, not to commit ourselves to, anything until we can see proof of it. The method works well enough for the verification of scientific theory but it does not work in the dimension of reality that lies beyond appearances. There we must commit ourselves before we see God, because without that commitment there is no purity of heart, no undivided consciousness, and only the pure of heart can see God. The commitment must be unconditional, innocent of self-interest, childlike, 'a condition of complete simplicity demanding not less than everything'. It only requires a little experience of meditation to understand those words of Dame Julian [of Norwich]. (PC, p.93)

The First Letter of
Saint Peter

✦ ✦

So come to him, our living Stone – the stone rejected by
men but choice and precious in the sight of God. Come,
and let yourselves be built, as living stones, into a spiritual temple; become a holy priesthood, to offer spiritual
sacrifices acceptable to God, through Jesus Christ . . . You
are a chosen race, a royal priesthood, a dedicated nation,
and a people claimed by God for his own, to proclaim
the triumphs of him who has called you out of darkness
into his marvellous light. You are now the people of
God, who once were not his people; outside his mercy
once, you have now received his mercy. (1 Pet 2: 4–6,
9–10)

Every life has a divine significance. Every life has a divine
potential. In meditating we open our lives to that significance and to that potential and in that opening we are
swept beyond ourselves into the creative energy of God.
The way is the way of humility, to say our word and to say
it faithfully and to say it every morning and every evening.
It is the way of simplicity, to surrender complexity, to surrender dividedness and to stay with the divine oneness of
God. And it is the way of faithfulness, of constancy. We are
faithful to our own destiny in God. We are faithful to the
realisation that we can only be in God. (HC, p.58)

The ultimate value is God's love for each of us as well as

for all creation. These two are really one, as God, being one, does not divide his love. He loves all or nothing, and does so equally because he loves absolutely. Human value – and God's love for us gives us this value – is personal. Faith, which is the transcendent point of encountering this love, must also be utterly personal. It must be your own faith, not somebody else's belief you have inherited or absorbed. You will encounter this faith in your own heart and in doing so meet God in the heart of Jesus.

Every time we meditate, alone or in a group, we respond to this call from darkness into his marvellous light. (WF, pp.50–51)

＋━ ━＋

In his own person he carried our sins to the gibbet, so that we might cease to live for sin and begin to live for righteousness. (1 Pet. 2: 24)

Meditation is the great way of purification. Every time we say our mantra, we purify, we clarify our spirit. The process of meditation over a lifetime is the restoration of our spirit to its natural translucency. So often, when we look into our spirit, we see only ourselves. Our spirit is like a mirror and all we see is our own reflection. But the glass must be cleared and cleansed. It is as though the other side of the glass is covered with the sum total of the dross and trivia of a lifetime, with all the images that we have accumulated. Meditation is a cleansing of the glass so that when we look *at* it we see right *through* it. We see reality unimpeded by any reflection of ourselves. We have to meditate every day, every morning and evening, because we are always accumulating more limiting dross and images. The wonder of the life of Jesus and his message to us is that our spirit need not be constrained by any limits whatsoever. Each of us is called to unlimited development, to expansion and to utter freedom as we soar to total union with God. (HC. p.62)

+>= =<+.

'Whoever loves life . . . must turn from wrong and do good, seek peace and pursue it.' (1 Pet. 3: 10–11)

When we meditate, we turn away from all illusion, from all images, from all fear, and we turn to God himself. We start by returning to our own heart and the extraordinary thing is that, as we are filled with his glory, with his love, there is no longer any place for us to stand, even in our own hearts. In meditation we are truly lost in the light of his glory, and it is when we are lost in that light that we become the light. There is a lot of darkness in our world. It is in desperate need of light, of men and women of light. And our pilgrimage of selflessness, which is also one of discipline, is a pilgrimage into the light. That is why when we meditate we must learn the discipline to sit perfectly still and to say the mantra with perfect attention: to leave everything of self behind. We must come to the place where we have no place. We must come directly to the light so that we become the light.

. . . To meditate is to have life, to be converted, to seek peace, not just for ourselves but for all. (HC, pp.63, 64)

The First Letter of
Saint John

⊷ ⊶

Our theme is the word of life. This life was made visible;
we have seen it and bear our testimony; we here declare
to you the eternal life which dwelt with the Father and
was made visible to us. What we have seen and heard
we declare to you, so that you and we together may
share in a common life, that life we share with the Father
and his Son Jesus Christ ... Here is the message we
heard from him, and pass on to you: that God is light,
and in him there is no darkness at all. (1 John 1: 1–5)

It is our call as Christians to come into that light and so to
leave utterly behind all darkness. The way to that light is
the way of humility in silence; the way of the mantra. (HC,
p.11)

⊷ ⊶

You need no other teacher, but learn all you need to
know from his initiation, which is real and no illusion.
As he taught you, then, dwell in him. (1 John 2: 27)

Just as the centre of Jesus' consciousness is his Father, so
our centre of consciousness must be Jesus. When we have
turned wholly towards him as the central reality of our life
to which everything else is relative, then his full, unified
consciousness dawns within us. In our loving union with

him at the centre, and consequently at all levels of our being, we know him as the One Teacher – we know it though it is beyond knowledge because, as St Paul proclaims to us, 'We have the mind of Christ'. There is the one Lord and he is the only teacher, the *sadguru*. (LH, p.55)

+━━ ━━+

What we shall be has not yet been disclosed, but we know that when it is disclosed we shall be like him, because we shall see him as he is. (1 John 3: 2)

There is an immortal power, the 'strength' of God, in this sensitivity. And that is why we cannot enter the new vision without finding a harmony with the basic structure of reality, without being sensitive to the truth that the underpinning reality of everything we see is God.

... It is in this sense that meditation is rightly called a way of wisdom, a way of vision. Wisdom is more than the knowledge derived from accumulated experience. Vision is more than the power to visualise. To be wise we must learn to know with the heart. To see we must learn to see with the eyes of the heart – with love. (PC, pp.91, 92)

+━━ ━━+

The man who does not love is still in the realm of death, for everyone who hates his brother is a murderer, and no murderer, as you know, has eternal life dwelling within him. It is by this that we know what love is: that Christ laid down his life for us. And we in our turn are bound to lay down our lives for our brothers. (1 John 3: 15–16)

Now as Christian thinkers or apologists we speak of God as supreme reality, but as ordinary Christian human beings with hearts of flesh, we say and know that God is Love. This is to say the same thing but from a deeper, more integrated and fully conscious perception. We experience reality because we are capable of loving and of being loved. To know love and to be known in love is to know reality . . .

. . . Our commitment to meditation is our openness to the peace of God's redemptive love, our total acceptance of it, our abandonment of self-fixation and our commitment to self-giving. (HC, pp.24, 25)

+>= =<+

Dear friends, let us love one another, because love is from God. Everyone who loves is a child of God and knows God, but the unloving know nothing of God. For God is love; and his love was disclosed to us in this, that he sent his only Son into the world to bring us life. The love I speak of is not our love for God, but the love he showed to us in sending his Son as the remedy for the defilement of our sins. If God thus loved us, dear friends, we in turn are bound to love one another . . . his love is brought to perfection within us. Here is the proof that we dwell in him and he dwells in us: he has imparted his Spirit to us. (1 John 4: 7–13)

Love evokes a spirit of joy in life; it evokes its variety, its unexpectedness, its colour. And the more generously we allow this spirit of love to expand within us, the more we become other-centred; the more we find our perfection in the other, our fulfilment in the other. It is in this experience that we let go of self-consciousness and discover our real consciousness. We discover it in contact with another consciousness. Out of this encounter comes the creative energy that enables us to work selflessly, lovingly. (HC, p.24)

+>= =<+

> If a man says 'I love God' while hating his brother, he
> is a liar. If he does not love the brother whom he has
> seen, it cannot be that he loves God whom he has not
> seen. And indeed this command comes to us from Christ
> himself: that he who loves God must also love his
> brother. (1 John 4: 19–21)

... Let us be quite clear what St John is saying, namely that
we cannot love God *or* our neighbour. We love both or
neither ...

In meditation we develop our capacity to turn our whole
being towards the Other. We learn to let our neighbour be
just as we learn to let God be. We learn not to manipulate
our neighbour but rather to reverence him, to reverence his
importance, the wonder of his being; in other words, we
learn to love him. Because of this, prayer is the great school
of community. In and through a common seriousness and
perseverance in prayer we realise the true glory of Christian
community as a fraternity of the anointed, living together
in profound and loving mutual respect. (WS, p.78)

＋━ ━＋

> If he does not love his brother whom he has seen, it
> cannot be that he loves God whom he has not seen. And
> indeed this command comes to us from Christ himself:
> that he who loves God must also love his brother.

There can be no other way to communicate the mystery of
the Christian experience because that mystery is one of a
person: the person of Jesus whose full personhood already
involves and contains ours. Again, this can sound very
abstract until you approach it from the model of your own
experience of love: in your marriage, your family, your
friendships. If you try to approach prayer by the model of
love I have been suggesting without rooting it in your own

experience of human love you will be dealing with shadows and phantoms. Prayer is concerned with the reality and actuality of persons. (CL, p.97)

━━   ━━

He who believes in the Son of God has this testimony in his own heart . . . The witness is this: that God has given us eternal life, and that this life is found in his Son. (1 John 5: 10, 11)

So many lives are lived by responding to other people's goals for us, society's goals for us, the advertising industry's goals for us. Christian revelation says that each of us is summoned to respond directly to the fullness of our own life in the mystery of God. How then are we to break out of the enclosed circle of inauthenticity and its consequent lifelessness? There is only one way and it is the basic message of the New Testament: to be fully open to the gift of eternal life. (WF, p.38)

The Revelation of
John

+>= =<+

I heard a loud voice, proclaiming from the throne: 'Now
at last God has his dwelling among men! He will dwell
among them and they shall be his people, and God
himself will be with them. He will wipe away every tear
from their eyes, there shall be an end to death and to
mourning and crying and pain; for the old order has
passed away!' (Rev. 21: 3–4)

We are led to meditate because we are convinced that the
old order has passed away and because we are convinced
that God does dwell among us. In faith we are convinced
that God dwells in our hearts. And if only we will take the
trouble and the time, each of us is invited to *find* God in
our hearts. Everyone is invited to undertake the journey
and then all that is required is that we stay on it. (WU, p.54)

Epilogue

The poverty and joy of our word leads us into the sea of the reality of God and, once there, it keeps us simply in the current of the Spirit and leads us to a place unknown to us where we know ourselves in him, in his eternal now. (PC, p.118)

I have talked a lot and sometimes quite elaborately. But let me end by reminding you that nothing can be said about prayer that can at the same time describe its utter fullness and its utter simplicity. I suggest you now forget most of what I have said except the two words 'simplicity' and 'faith' – and both of these are summed up in the practice of the one word that will allow you to be led by the Spirit. I have not suggested to you that the simplicity is easy to reach or the faith easy to maintain. But let me remind you again that this condition of whole-hearted openness to love is the condition to which you and I and every human being is called. It demands everything. But in the end all you will lose are your limitations. So may we 'attain to fullness of being, the fullness of God himself' (Eph. 3: 19). (CL, p.114)

Appendix 1:
New Testament Sources

+══ ══+

Daily *lectio divina*, a slow reading of the Sacred Scriptures, is central to a life of prayer. The Word of God leads to a discovery of the Spirit more fully in ourselves, in each other, and in all of creation. It also contributes to a deeper appreciation of the daily practice of meditation. Our daily meditation, in turn, leads us to a deeper appreciation of the Word of God as expressed in our Sacred Scriptures, as well as of the wisdom found in the scriptures of other traditions.

The following passages were marked by John Main in his personal copy of the New Testament (New English Bible translation). Meditators will find these passages especially meaningful in light of Father John's commentaries on them, and in his teaching on meditation.

ST MATTHEW'S GOSPEL

Chapter	1	Verses	7–14;
			19–21;
			33–34;
			13–14
	10		7–8
	13		7–8
	16		24–26
	24		42

ST MARK'S GOSPEL

Chapter	8	Verses 34–36
	10	15

ST LUKE'S GOSPEL

Chapter	3	Verses	1–6
	5		16
	6		12
	9		23–24
	12		27–31
	13		18–19
	14		15–24

ST JOHN'S GOSPEL

Chapter	1	Verses 14; 29–34
	3	3–8;
		13–17
	4	13–14;
		23–24

St Paul's Letter to the
Ephesians

Chapter	1	Verses	1; 3–10;
			17–33
	2		6–7;
			12–14;
			17–22
	3		4; 9;
			12–13;
			14–21
	4		6–7;
			13–14
	5		15–18;
			25–33

St Paul's Letter to the
Philippians

Chapter	1	Verses	9–10;
			20–21
	2		5
	3		9;
			10–11; 21
	4		1; 7

St Paul's Letter to the
Colossians

Chapter	1	Verses	11–20;
			26–27
	2		1–5; 6–7;
			9–10; 20
	3		4; 9–11
	4		23

St Paul's First Letter to the
Thessalonians

| Chapter | 4 | Verses | 1 |

St Paul's Second Letter to
the Thessalonians

| Chapter | 2 | Verses 13–17 |

St Paul's First Letter to
Timothy

| Chapter | 4 | Verses 9–10 |

St Paul's Second Letter to
Timothy

Chapter	1	Verses	7–10
	2		1
	3		7

Hebrews

Chapter	6	Verses	1–6
	9		11–14
	10		19–20
	12		28–29

Letter to James

| Chapter | 3 | Verses 13 |
| | 5 | | 13–16 |

First Letter of Peter

Chapter	1	Verses 1; 4; 13–16
	2		1–10; 24
	3		4; 13–16
	4		6; 8

First Letter of St John

Chapter	2	Verses 24–25;
			28–29
	3		14–16; 18;
			23–24
	4		7–10
	5		11–12

Appendix 2:
Meditation Centres Worldwide

+=— =—+

INTERNATIONAL CENTRE
23 Kensington Square
London W8 5HN
England
Tel: 0171 937 4679
Fax: 0171 937 6790

AUSTRALIA
Christian Meditation Network
10 Grovesnor Road
Glen Iris, Victoria 3136
Tel: 03 822 4870

BELGIUM
Christelijk Meditatie Centrum
Beiaardlaam 1
1850 Grimbergen
Tel: 02 269 5071

CANADA
Meditatio
PO Box 552 Station NDG
Montreal, Quebec H4 3P9
Tel: 514 766 0475
Fax: 514 937 8178

INDIA
Christian Meditation Centre
1/1429 Bilathikulam Road
Calicut 673006
Kerala
Tel: 495 60395

IRELAND
Christian Meditation Centre
56 Meadow Grove
Blackrock, Cork
Tel: 021 357 249

NEW ZEALAND
Christian Meditation Centre
PO Box 139
Orewa
Tel: 0642 63 891

PHILIPPINES
Christian Meditation Centre
5/f Chronicle Building
Cor. Tektite Road
Pasig, M. Manila
Tel: 02 633 3364
Fax: 02 632 3104

SINGAPORE
Christian Meditation Centre
Holy Family Church
6 Chapel Road
Singapore 1542
Tel: 344 0046

UNITED KINGDOM
Christian Meditation Centre
29 Campden Hill
London W8 7DX
Tel: 0171 937 0014
Fax: 0171 937 6790

THAILAND
Christian Meditation Centre
51/1 Sedsiri Road
Bangkok 10400
Tel: 271 3295

UNITED STATES
John Main Institute
7315 Brookville Road
Chevy Chase, MD 20815
Tel: 301 652 8635

Christian Meditation Centre
1080 West Irving Park Road
Roselle. IL 60172
Tel: 708 351 2613

Hesed Community
3745 Elston Avenue
Oakland
San Francisco
California 94602
Tel: 415 482 5573

Christian Meditation Centre
322 E. 94th Street
New York, NY 10128
Tel: 212–831–5710

Appendix 3:
WCCM on the Internet: FTP and The World Wide Web

WCCM.Archive Index

The World Community for Christian Meditation, in collaboration with The Merton Research Institute located at Marshall University (WV, USA), now offers documents and information via the Internet. The index of the WCCM archive identifies the sites to access the archives, the main directory of the archive, its subdirectories, the pathnames to the subdirectories, and the filenames of the available documents. The index of files and all individual files may be accessed using anonymous FTP or the WWW at the following URLs:

ftp://byrd.mu.wvnet.edu pub/merton wccm/
http://www.marshall.edu/~stepp/vri/merton/WCCM.html

The procedure for direct access by anonymous ftp is:

ftp byrd.mu.wvnet.edu
login anonymous
password: user's Internet address
cd pathname
get ⟨filename⟩ [*Type filename you wish to retrieve*]
quit

To retrieve files, type pathnames and filenames exactly as they appear here.

The WCCM MAIN DIRECTORY points users to Newsletters, Biographies, Schedules, Catalogues, Meditation Centres and contact people, John Main Seminar information, How To Meditate, Oblate information, and other files.

WCCM.Forum

The WCCM.Forum is an outgrowth of the WCCM.Archive. The expressed and sole purpose of the WCCM.Forum is to provide a place for substantive discussion on the daily practice of Christian Meditation as taught by John Main, the works of John Main and Laurence Freeman, and the work of the WCCM in general.

To join the WCCM.Forum one must be a present member of Merton-L or, if not, subscribe to it. To subscribe to Merton-L, send email to:

LISTSERV@WVNVM.WVNET.EDU

containing the following lines of text:

SUBSCRIBE MERTON-L YOURNAME
[*substituting your real full name for YOURNAME, of course*]
SET MERTON-L TOPICS: +T6

The automated Welcome Message will offer further details and easy-to-follow instructions.

For more Internet information contact:

Gregory Ryan
Internet e-mail: gjryan@aol.com

Bibliography

+≻= =≺+

Christian Meditation: The Gethsemani Talks. Benedictine Priory, Montreal, 1983.

Community of Love. Darton, Longman and Todd, 1990.

Death the Inner Journey. Benedictine Priory, Montreal, 1983.

The Heart of Creation. Darton, Longman and Todd, 1988.

Letters from the Heart: Christian monasticism and the renewal of community. Crossroad, New York, 1982; reprinted 1984.

Moment of Christ. Darton, Longman and Todd, 1984; Crossroad, New York, 1984.

The Present Christ. Darton, Longman and Todd, 1985; Crossroad, New York, 1985.

The Way of Unknowing. Darton, Longman and Todd, 1989; Crossroad, New York, 1989.

Word Into Silence. Darton, Longman and Todd, 1980; Paulist Press, New York, 1981.

Word Made Flesh. Darton, Longman and Todd, 1993; Crossroad, 1993.